Investing Demystified: A Beginner's Guide to Building Wealth in the Stock Market

Alex Thompson

Published by Side Hustle Success, 2023.

INVESTING DEMYSTIFIED: A BEGINNER'S GUIDE TO BUILDING WEALTH IN THE STOCK MARKET

First edition. July 27, 2023.

ISBN: 979-8223167303

Written by Alex Thompson.

Also by Alex Thompson

Alex on Finance

Financial Freedom Roadmap - Achieving Early Retirement through the FIRE Movement

The Art of Strategic Innovation

Beyond Cash - The Evolution of Digital Payment Systems and the Future of Money

Preserving Wealth in Inflationary Times - Strategies for Protecting Your Financial Future

Standalone

Side Hustle Success: Unlocking Your Entrepreneurial Potential

Side Hustle Success: The Ultimate Guide to Passive and Financial Freedom

Mastering the Markets: Advanced Trading Strategies for Success and Ethical Trading Practices

Financial Fortitude

Mastering the Art of Upselling

The Financial Bullet Blueprint

Investing Demystified: A Beginner's Guide to Building Wealth in the Stock Market

Table of Contents

Chapter 1: The World of Investing

What is Investing and Why It Matters for Your Financial Future

Investing is the art and science of putting your money to work to generate potential returns over time. Rather than letting your money sit idle, investing allows you to grow your wealth by participating in the growth of various assets, such as stocks, bonds, real estate, and more. While investing carries certain risks, it offers the potential for higher returns compared to traditional savings accounts.

- **The Importance of Investing**

- Building Wealth: Investing provides an opportunity to accumulate wealth and achieve financial goals.
- Beating Inflation: Inflation erodes the purchasing power of money; investing helps outpace inflation and maintain real value.
- Retirement Planning: Investing is essential for creating a secure financial future during retirement.
- Funding Goals: Whether it's buying a house, funding education, or starting a business, investing can help achieve specific financial goals.

- **Understanding Risk and Return**

- Risk: All investments carry some level of risk. Understanding and managing risk is crucial to successful investing.
- Return: Potential return is the reward for taking on investment risk. Different assets offer varying levels of potential returns.

- **Types of Investments**

- Stocks: Owning a share in a company entitles you to a portion of its profits and assets.
- Bonds: Lending money to a government or corporation in exchange for regular interest payments.
- Mutual Funds: Pools of money from multiple investors, invested in a diversified portfolio of stocks and/or bonds.
- Real Estate: Investing in properties for rental income or potential appreciation.
- Commodities: Investing in physical goods like gold, oil, or agricultural products.

- **The Power of Compounding**

- Time and Compound Interest: The longer your money is invested, the more it benefits from compounding.
- Reinvesting Dividends: Reinvesting dividends and returns can significantly boost your investment growth.

- **Understanding Your Risk Tolerance**

- Conservative vs. Aggressive Investors: Assessing your risk tolerance helps determine your investment approach.
- Aligning Investments with Goals: Different financial goals may require different risk levels.

As you embark on your investment journey, it's essential to educate yourself about the various investment options and their potential risks and rewards. Remember that investing is a long-term endeavor, and making well-informed decisions based on your financial goals will greatly influence your path to building wealth in the stock market and other assets.

Understanding Risk and Return in Different Investment Vehicles

When investing, it's crucial to comprehend the relationship between risk and return. Different investment vehicles offer varying levels of risk and potential return, and finding the right balance is essential to achieving your financial goals.

- **Risk and Its Types**

- Market Risk: The risk of fluctuations in the overall market that can affect all investments.
- Company/Issuer Risk: Specific to individual stocks and bonds, it pertains to the financial health and performance of a particular company or issuer.
- Credit Risk: The possibility of bond issuers defaulting on interest or principal payments.
- Inflation Risk: The risk that inflation will erode the purchasing power of investment returns.
- Liquidity Risk: The difficulty of selling an investment quickly without significantly impacting its price.

- **Return and Its Components**

- Capital Appreciation: The increase in the value of an investment over its purchase price.
- Dividends and Interest: Periodic payments from stocks or bonds, respectively, to investors.
- Rental Income: Returns from real estate investments through rental payments.

- **Risk-Return Tradeoff**

- Higher Risk, Higher Potential Return: Investments with higher risk tend to offer the potential for greater returns.
- Lower Risk, Lower Potential Return: Safer investments

generally come with lower return expectations.

- **Different Investment Vehicles and Their Risk-Return Profiles**

- Stocks: Historically, stocks have provided the highest returns among major asset classes but come with higher volatility.
- Bonds: Generally considered safer than stocks, bonds offer lower but more predictable returns.
- Mutual Funds and ETFs: Diversified portfolios that spread risk across various assets, offering a balanced risk-return profile.
- Real Estate: Potential for long-term appreciation and rental income but subject to market fluctuations.
- Commodities: Can be highly volatile, and returns are influenced by supply and demand factors.

- **Risk Tolerance and Investment Strategy**

- Conservative Investors: May prefer lower-risk investments, prioritizing capital preservation over high returns.
- Moderate Investors: Willing to take on some risk for the potential of higher returns, but also value stability.
- Aggressive Investors: Comfortable with higher risk to pursue the potential for significant long-term growth.

- **Diversification as Risk Mitigation**

- Spreading Risk: Diversifying across various asset classes and industries can reduce overall portfolio risk.
- Building Resilience: Diversification helps protect against severe losses from the poor performance of a single investment.

Understanding the risk-return characteristics of different investment options empowers you to make informed decisions that align with your risk tolerance and financial objectives. Remember that risk is an inherent part of investing, and achieving higher returns often requires taking on greater risk. Balancing risk and return is a key aspect of successful wealth accumulation in the stock market and other investment avenues.

Overview of Stocks, Bonds, Mutual Funds, and Other Assets

Before delving into the world of investing, it's essential to familiarize yourself with the primary investment vehicles available. Each asset class has distinct characteristics, risk profiles, and potential returns, offering investors a range of options to diversify their portfolios.

- **Stocks**

- Ownership: Stocks represent ownership in a company, making investors partial owners with a claim to its assets and earnings.
- Potential Returns: Stocks have historically provided higher returns than other asset classes, but they are also more volatile.
- Dividends: Some companies pay dividends, distributing a portion of their profits to shareholders regularly.
- Growth Stocks: Companies expected to have above-average growth rates; their stock prices may increase significantly over time.
- Value Stocks: Shares of companies perceived to be undervalued based on fundamental analysis, with potential for future growth.

- **Bonds**

- Debt Investment: Bonds are debt securities where investors lend money to governments or corporations for a predetermined period.
- Fixed Income: Bonds pay periodic interest (coupon payments) to investors, providing a predictable income stream.
- Maturity: Bonds have specific maturity dates when the principal amount is repaid to the bondholders.
- Types: Government bonds, corporate bonds, municipal bonds, and treasury bonds are common bond categories.

- **Mutual Funds**

- Pooled Investments: Mutual funds pool money from multiple investors to invest in a diversified portfolio of stocks, bonds, or both.
- Professional Management: Managed by fund managers who make investment decisions on behalf of the investors.
- Diversification: Mutual funds offer instant diversification across multiple securities, reducing individual investment risk.
- Types: Equity funds, bond funds, index funds, sector funds, and target-date funds, among others.

- **Exchange-Traded Funds (ETFs)**

- Similarities to Mutual Funds: ETFs are also pooled investments offering diversification and professional management.
- Trade on Exchanges: ETF shares trade on stock exchanges like individual stocks, with prices fluctuating throughout the trading day.
- Lower Expenses: ETFs often have lower expense ratios

compared to traditional mutual funds.

- **Real Estate Investment Trusts (REITs)**

- Real Estate Ownership: REITs invest in income-generating real estate properties, such as commercial buildings, apartments, or malls.
- Regular Income: They are required to distribute a significant portion of their earnings to shareholders as dividends.
- Stock Market Presence: REITs are publicly traded on exchanges like stocks.

- **Commodities**

- Physical Goods: Commodities are raw materials or primary agricultural products traded in standardized contracts.
- Examples: Gold, silver, oil, natural gas, wheat, corn, etc.
- Diversification Benefit: Commodities can act as a hedge against inflation and diversify a portfolio.

As an investor, understanding the characteristics of different assets is vital for constructing a well-balanced portfolio tailored to your financial goals and risk tolerance. Combining various asset classes can help spread risk, enhance returns, and optimize the potential for long-term wealth accumulation in the stock market and beyond.

Introducing the Concept of Compounding and Its Power in Wealth Building

Compounding is a fundamental concept in investing that can significantly amplify wealth-building potential over time. It allows investors to earn returns not only on their initial investment but also on the accumulated earnings from previous periods. As the investment grows, the returns generated also increase, leading to exponential growth over the long term.

- **How Compounding Works**

- Starting Principal: When you invest an initial amount, it becomes your starting principal.
- Investment Returns: Over time, your investment generates returns, such as dividends, interest, or capital gains.
- Reinvestment: Instead of withdrawing these returns, you reinvest them back into the original investment.

- **The Power of Time**

- Longer Investment Horizon: The longer you keep your money invested, the more time it has to compound and grow.
- Snowball Effect: As compounding continues, the growth becomes increasingly significant, resembling a snowball rolling downhill.

- **The Rule of 72**

- Quick Estimation: The Rule of 72 is a simple formula to estimate how long it takes an investment to double in value.
- Calculation: Divide 72 by the annual rate of return to approximate the number of years for doubling.

- **Example of Compounding**

- Starting with $10,000: Assume you invest $10,000 in an asset with an average annual return of 8%.
- After 10 years: Your investment grows to approximately $21,589.

- After 20 years: Your investment reaches approximately $46,610.
- After 30 years: Your investment soars to approximately $100,627.

- **Consistency is Key**

- Regular Contributions: Adding to your investment regularly amplifies the power of compounding.
- Benefits of Dollar-Cost Averaging: Dollar-cost averaging involves investing fixed amounts at regular intervals, buying more shares when prices are low and fewer when prices are high.

- **Start Early, Start Now**

- Advantage of Youth: The earlier you begin investing, the more time compounding has to work in your favor.
- Even Small Amounts Help: Regular contributions, no matter how small, can lead to substantial growth over time.

- **The Impact on Long-Term Wealth Building**

- Leveraging Longevity: Compounding is particularly effective for long-term investment goals, such as retirement planning.
- Lessens the Burden: By harnessing the power of compounding, you may require smaller contributions to achieve your financial objectives.

Understanding the concept of compounding and its potential to accelerate wealth-building underscores the importance of starting early and staying invested for the long term. Consistency, patience, and the benefits of time are key factors in maximizing the power of compounding and achieving your financial aspirations in the stock market and other investment avenues.

Chapter 2: Getting Started with Stocks

What are Stocks and How They Work

Stocks, also known as shares or equities, represent ownership in a company. When you own stocks of a company, you become a shareholder, giving you certain rights and entitlements in that business. Understanding how stocks work is essential for any investor venturing into the stock market.

- **Ownership and Shareholders**

- Owning a Piece of the Company: When you buy stocks, you are purchasing a portion of the company's ownership.
- Shareholders' Rights: As a shareholder, you have the right to vote in company decisions, attend shareholder meetings, and receive dividends if the company distributes profits.

- **How Stocks are Issued**

- Initial Public Offering (IPO): When a private company decides to go public, it conducts an IPO, issuing shares to the public for the first time.
- Secondary Offerings: Companies may issue additional shares to raise more capital after the IPO.

- **Stock Exchanges and Trading**

- Stock Exchanges: Stocks are traded on stock exchanges, which are centralized marketplaces for buying and selling securities.
- Examples: New York Stock Exchange (NYSE), Nasdaq, London Stock Exchange (LSE), Tokyo Stock Exchange

(TSE), etc.

- Stock Ticker Symbols: Each company listed on an exchange has a unique ticker symbol used for identification during trading.

- **How Stock Prices are Determined**

- Supply and Demand: Stock prices fluctuate based on the forces of supply and demand in the market.
- Bid and Ask Prices: The highest price a buyer is willing to pay (bid) and the lowest price a seller is willing to accept (ask) determine the stock's current price.

- **Types of Stocks**

- Common Stocks: Most common type, representing basic ownership and voting rights in the company.
- Preferred Stocks: Holders receive preferential treatment for dividends and in case of company liquidation but usually do not have voting rights.

- **Stock Indices**

- Market Performance Measurement: Stock indices track the performance of a group of stocks, reflecting the overall market sentiment or specific industry performance.
- Examples: S&P 500, Dow Jones Industrial Average (DJIA), Nasdaq Composite, FTSE 100, etc.

- **How Stocks Generate Returns**

- Capital Gains: If the stock price increases, you can sell the stock at a higher price than what you initially paid, resulting

in a capital gain.
- Dividends: Some companies distribute a portion of their profits to shareholders as dividends, providing a regular income stream.

- **Risks of Investing in Stocks**

- Market Volatility: Stock prices can be highly volatile, influenced by various factors, including economic conditions and company performance.
- Individual Company Risk: The performance of a single company can significantly impact the value of its stock.

Understanding the fundamentals of stocks is crucial before investing in individual companies. Stocks offer an opportunity to participate in a company's growth and success, but they also carry risks. Diversification and conducting research are essential strategies to manage risk and build a well-rounded portfolio in the stock market.

Different Types of Stocks (Common vs. Preferred) and Their Characteristics

When investing in stocks, it's important to be aware of the two main types of stocks available: common stocks and preferred stocks. Each type comes with its own set of characteristics and rights, offering investors various options based on their investment objectives and risk tolerance.

- **Common Stocks**

- Ownership and Voting Rights: Common stockholders have ownership in the company and typically possess voting rights in shareholder meetings. Each share usually carries one vote, allowing shareholders to influence certain company decisions.

- Dividends: Companies may distribute dividends to common shareholders, but the payment is not guaranteed and depends on the company's financial performance and management's discretion.
- Capital Appreciation: Common stocks offer the potential for capital appreciation, where the stock price increases over time, allowing investors to sell at a profit.
- Risk and Return: Common stocks are more volatile compared to preferred stocks, offering potentially higher returns but also carrying a higher level of risk.

- **Preferred Stocks**

- Dividends: Preferred stockholders receive fixed dividends, typically at a predetermined rate. These dividends are paid before common shareholders receive theirs, providing a degree of income stability.
- No Voting Rights or Limited Voting Rights: In most cases, preferred shareholders do not have voting rights, or their voting rights are limited. They usually don't have a say in company decisions like common shareholders do.
- Capital Appreciation: Preferred stocks have a fixed par value, which means their price doesn't fluctuate like common stocks. As a result, preferred stocks generally offer limited capital appreciation potential.
- Priority in Liquidation: In the event of company liquidation, preferred shareholders have a higher claim on the company's assets than common shareholders, which can provide some protection.

- **Preference in Dividends**

- Cumulative Preferred Stock: If the company skips a dividend payment, cumulative preferred shareholders are entitled to receive unpaid dividends in the future before any common stock dividends are paid.
- Non-Cumulative Preferred Stock: If the company skips a dividend payment, non-cumulative preferred shareholders do not have the right to claim unpaid dividends.

- **Conversion Feature**
    - Some preferred stocks come with a conversion feature that allows shareholders to convert their preferred shares into a predetermined number of common shares. This feature offers the potential to benefit from capital appreciation if the common stock price rises.
- **Risk and Reward Tradeoff**

- Preferred stocks are generally considered less risky than common stocks due to their fixed dividend payments and higher priority in liquidation.
- However, the tradeoff is that preferred stocks offer limited upside potential compared to common stocks.

Investors must carefully consider their financial objectives, risk tolerance, and income requirements when choosing between common and preferred stocks. Common stocks offer growth potential but come with higher risk and market volatility. Preferred stocks, on the other hand, provide a more stable income stream but with limited potential for capital appreciation. Diversification and a balanced approach to including both types of stocks in a portfolio can help achieve a well-rounded investment strategy in the stock market.

Researching and Selecting Individual Stocks

Investing in individual stocks requires thorough research and analysis to make informed decisions. While it can be rewarding, it also carries higher risk compared to investing in diversified funds. Here are some essential steps to research and select individual stocks:

- **Understand Your Investment Goals and Risk Tolerance**

- Determine your investment objectives, whether it's long-term growth, income, or a combination of both.
- Assess your risk tolerance to gauge how much volatility and potential loss you can handle.

- **Fundamental Analysis**

- Study the Company: Examine the company's financial health, business model, competitive advantage, and management team.
- Financial Statements: Review the company's income statement, balance sheet, and cash flow statement to understand its financial performance and stability.
- Ratios and Metrics: Utilize key financial ratios like Price-to-Earnings (P/E), Price-to-Book (P/B), and Debt-to-Equity (D/E) to assess valuation and financial strength.

- **Technical Analysis**

- Price Trends: Analyze historical price charts to identify trends, support and resistance levels, and potential entry and exit points.
- Volume: Consider trading volume as an indicator of market interest and liquidity.
- Moving Averages: Use moving averages to understand price momentum and potential trend reversals.

- **Industry and Market Analysis**

- Sector Performance: Analyze the performance of the industry or sector the company operates in to understand its growth prospects and challenges.
- Economic Factors: Consider broader economic trends that may impact the company's business.

- **Competitive Landscape**

- Identify Competitors: Understand the company's position relative to its competitors.
- Competitive Advantage: Assess the company's unique strengths and advantages that set it apart from others in the industry.

- **Company News and Events**

- Stay Informed: Monitor news and events related to the company, such as product launches, mergers, acquisitions, and leadership changes.
- Earnings Reports: Pay attention to quarterly and annual earnings reports, as they can significantly influence stock prices.

- **Diversification**

- Avoid Overconcentration: Diversify your stock portfolio across different companies, industries, and regions to spread risk.
- Consider Sectors: Allocate your investments across sectors to reduce the impact of industry-specific risks.

- **Seek Professional Advice**
    - If unsure about stock selection or investing in general, consider consulting a financial advisor who can offer personalized guidance based on your financial situation and goals.

Remember that investing in individual stocks requires time and effort to research, analyze, and monitor your investments actively. Be prepared to continuously review your holdings, adapt to changing market conditions, and make necessary adjustments to your portfolio. Additionally, always be mindful of the risks associated with investing in individual stocks and balance your stock picks with other diversified investment options in your portfolio.

Introduction to Stock Exchanges and How to Place a Trade

Stock exchanges are the primary marketplaces where stocks and other securities are bought and sold. Understanding how stock exchanges work and how to place a trade is essential for investors looking to enter the stock market.

- **How Stock Exchanges Work**

- Centralized Marketplaces: Stock exchanges act as centralized platforms where buyers and sellers come together to trade stocks.
- Listed Companies: Companies wishing to trade their shares on an exchange must meet specific requirements and regulations set by the exchange.
- Price Discovery: Stock exchanges facilitate price discovery, where the supply and demand for a stock determine its market price.

- **Major Stock Exchanges**

- New York Stock Exchange (NYSE): One of the largest and most well-known stock exchanges in the world, located on Wall Street in New York City.
- Nasdaq: An electronic exchange known for listing many technology and growth-oriented companies.
- London Stock Exchange (LSE): One of the oldest stock exchanges, located in London, UK.
- Tokyo Stock Exchange (TSE): The largest stock exchange in Japan.

- **Placing a Trade**

- Brokerage Account: To buy and sell stocks on a stock exchange, you'll need a brokerage account with a licensed brokerage firm.
- Selecting a Stock: Decide on the stock you want to buy based on your research and analysis.
- Types of Orders:

- Market Order: Buy or sell a stock at the current market price.
- Limit Order: Specify the price at which you are willing to buy or sell the stock. It will execute only if the stock reaches that price or better.
- Stop Order: Set a trigger price; once the stock reaches that price, a market order is executed.

- Number of Shares: Determine the number of shares you wish to buy or sell.

- **Order Execution**

- Order Routing: When you place a trade with your brokerage, they will route the order to the appropriate stock exchange.

- Bid and Ask: Your order will be matched with the best available bid or ask price in the market.

- **Trading Hours**

- Stock exchanges have specific trading hours during which orders are executed.
- Pre-Market and After-Hours Trading: Some exchanges offer extended trading hours outside regular market hours, but liquidity may be lower during these times.

- **Fees and Costs**

- Commissions: Brokers charge a commission or a fee for executing trades on your behalf.
- Other Costs: Consider other expenses like account maintenance fees, inactivity fees, and margin interest rates, if applicable.

- **Monitoring Your Portfolio**
    - After executing a trade, regularly monitor your portfolio's performance and stay updated on news and events that may impact your investments.

Placing a trade on a stock exchange is a straightforward process with the help of a brokerage account. However, remember that stock prices can be volatile, and it's essential to exercise caution and patience while making investment decisions. Proper research, understanding the mechanics of stock exchanges, and continuous monitoring will contribute to a more successful and informed investing experience in the stock market.

Chapter 3: Bonds and Fixed-Income Investments

Explaining Bonds and How They Differ from Stocks

Bonds are fixed-income investments that differ significantly from stocks in terms of their structure, risk-return profile, and ownership characteristics. Understanding the nature of bonds and their distinctions from stocks is crucial for constructing a well-balanced investment portfolio.

- **Definition of Bonds**

- Debt Securities: Bonds represent loans made by investors to governments, municipalities, or corporations.
- Fixed-Term: Bonds have a specific maturity date when the issuer repays the bond's face value to the investor.
- Regular Interest Payments: Issuers pay periodic interest (coupon payments) to bondholders at predetermined intervals.

- **Bondholders vs. Shareholders**

- Ownership: Bondholders are creditors of the issuer and do not own any part of the company, municipality, or government entity. In contrast, shareholders of a company have ownership rights.
- Risk and Reward: While both bondholders and shareholders face risks, bondholders have a more predictable income stream (through interest payments) and have a higher claim in case of issuer liquidation compared to shareholders.

- **Risk Profile**

- Higher Stability: Bonds are generally considered more stable than stocks due to their fixed-income nature and the preference given to bondholders in the event of bankruptcy or liquidation.
- Lower Potential Return: Bonds typically offer lower potential returns compared to stocks since they are debt instruments with a fixed interest rate.

- **Role in Diversification**

- Balancing Risk: Including bonds in a portfolio can help balance the risk of equity investments (stocks) and provide stability during volatile market conditions.
- Income Generation: Bonds can act as an income-generating asset, especially for investors seeking regular interest payments.

- **Types of Bonds**

- Government Bonds: Issued by national governments to finance public projects and operations. Examples include U.S. Treasury bonds and German Bunds.
- Municipal Bonds: Issued by state or local governments to fund infrastructure projects like schools, highways, or utilities.
- Corporate Bonds: Issued by corporations to raise capital for expansion, acquisitions, or operational needs.
- Treasury Inflation-Protected Securities (TIPS): Government bonds whose principal value adjusts based on inflation, providing a hedge against rising prices.

- **Credit Ratings**

- Evaluation of Risk: Bonds are assigned credit ratings by rating agencies, indicating the issuer's creditworthiness and the risk of default.
- Investment-Grade Bonds: Bonds with high credit ratings (e.g., AAA, AA, A) are considered lower risk.
- High-Yield Bonds (Junk Bonds): Bonds with lower credit ratings (e.g., BB, B, CCC) have higher default risk but offer higher yields to compensate investors for the added risk.

- **Interest Rate Sensitivity**

- Inverse Relationship: Bond prices have an inverse relationship with interest rates. When interest rates rise, bond prices typically fall, and vice versa.
- Duration: Duration measures a bond's sensitivity to interest rate changes.

Understanding the nature of bonds and their differences from stocks is essential for constructing a well-diversified investment portfolio that aligns with your financial goals and risk tolerance. Combining both asset classes can help reduce overall portfolio risk and provide a more stable income stream while also seeking potential growth opportunities in the stock market.

Understanding Bond Yields, Maturity, and Credit Ratings

When investing in bonds, it's essential to grasp key concepts like bond yields, maturity, and credit ratings, as they significantly impact the risk and return characteristics of bond investments.

- **Bond Yields**

- Definition: Bond yield refers to the annualized return an investor can expect to earn from a bond, considering its current market price, coupon rate, and time to maturity.
- Coupon Rate: The coupon rate is the fixed interest rate the bond pays annually (expressed as a percentage of the bond's face value).
- Current Yield: Current yield is the bond's annual interest payment divided by its current market price. It provides a snapshot of the bond's yield at its current price.

- **Yield to Maturity (YTM)**

- Definition: Yield to maturity represents the total return an investor can expect to receive if the bond is held until its maturity date.
- Factors Considered: YTM considers the bond's current price, coupon rate, time to maturity, and the reinvestment of coupon payments at the prevailing yield.

- **Maturity**

- Definition: Bond maturity refers to the date when the issuer repays the bond's face value to the bondholder. It marks the end of the bond's life.
- Short-Term vs. Long-Term Bonds: Bonds can have various maturities, ranging from short-term (less than one year) to long-term (10, 20, or 30 years).

- **Credit Ratings**

- Definition: Credit ratings assess the creditworthiness of bond issuers and their ability to meet their debt obligations.
- Rating Agencies: Independent rating agencies, such as

Standard & Poor's (S&P), Moody's, and Fitch, assign credit ratings to bonds.

- Investment-Grade Bonds: Bonds with higher credit ratings (e.g., AAA, AA, A) are considered investment-grade and have lower default risk.
- Speculative (Junk) Bonds: Bonds with lower credit ratings (e.g., BB, B, CCC) are considered speculative or junk bonds and have a higher risk of default.

- **Relationship Between Yields, Maturity, and Credit Ratings**

- Yield and Maturity: Generally, longer-term bonds offer higher yields than short-term bonds to compensate investors for the added time risk.
- Yield and Credit Ratings: Bonds with lower credit ratings tend to offer higher yields as they come with a higher risk of default.

- **Interest Rate Environment and Bond Prices**

- Inverse Relationship: Bond prices and interest rates have an inverse relationship. When interest rates rise, bond prices typically fall, and vice versa.
- Interest Rate Risk: Bonds with longer maturities are more sensitive to changes in interest rates, leading to greater interest rate risk.

- **Assessing Risk and Return**

- Balancing Risk: Investors should consider their risk tolerance and investment objectives when selecting bonds with the appropriate credit ratings and maturities.

- Diversification: Diversifying across different bond issuers, maturities, and credit ratings can help mitigate risk and optimize returns.

Understanding bond yields, maturity, and credit ratings is vital for evaluating the risk and potential return of bond investments. As an investor, it's essential to analyze bonds carefully based on these factors to build a balanced fixed-income portfolio that aligns with your financial goals and risk appetite. Additionally, monitoring interest rate changes and economic conditions is crucial to making informed decisions regarding bond investments in various interest rate environments.

Government Bonds vs. Corporate Bonds vs. Municipal Bonds

Bonds come in various forms, each with distinct characteristics and risk profiles. Understanding the differences between government bonds, corporate bonds, and municipal bonds can help investors make informed decisions when selecting fixed-income investments.

- **Government Bonds**

- Issuer: Government bonds are issued by national governments to raise funds for public projects, infrastructure development, and other governmental expenses.
- Credit Risk: Generally considered low-risk investments, as they are backed by the full faith and credit of the government.
- Types: Treasury bonds (long-term), Treasury notes (medium-term), and Treasury bills (short-term) are common types of government bonds in the United States.
- Yields: Government bonds tend to offer lower yields compared to other bonds due to their low credit risk.

- **Corporate Bonds**

- Issuer: Corporate bonds are issued by corporations to raise capital for various purposes, such as expansion, mergers, acquisitions, or working capital needs.
- Credit Risk: The creditworthiness of corporate bonds varies based on the financial health of the issuing company. Credit ratings help assess the default risk.
- Yields: Corporate bonds typically offer higher yields compared to government bonds due to the higher risk associated with corporate debt.

- **Municipal Bonds**

- Issuer: Municipal bonds (also known as munis) are issued by state or local governments and their agencies to fund public projects and infrastructure, such as schools, highways, and water facilities.
- Tax Advantages: Interest income from municipal bonds is often exempt from federal income tax. In some cases, it may also be exempt from state and local income taxes, making them attractive to investors in higher tax brackets.
- Credit Risk: Municipal bonds' credit risk varies based on the financial health of the issuing municipality. General obligation bonds are backed by the issuer's taxing power, while revenue bonds are supported by specific projects' revenue streams.
- Yields: Municipal bond yields are typically lower than corporate bond yields but may be comparable or slightly higher than government bond yields. The tax advantages may make them more attractive for certain investors.

- **Liquidity**

- Government bonds tend to be highly liquid, with active trading on major exchanges, such as the U.S. Treasury market.
- Corporate bonds also have reasonable liquidity, especially for bonds issued by large, well-established companies.
- Municipal bonds may have lower liquidity, particularly for bonds issued by smaller municipalities.

- **Considerations for Investors**

- Risk and Return: Government bonds offer lower risk and returns, while corporate bonds provide higher yields but with higher credit risk. Municipal bonds offer tax advantages but may have varying degrees of credit risk.
- Tax Implications: Investors should consider the tax implications of different bonds based on their individual tax situations.
- Diversification: Diversifying across various bond types can help manage risk in a fixed-income portfolio.

Investors should carefully assess their risk tolerance, investment goals, and tax situation when choosing between government bonds, corporate bonds, and municipal bonds. Each bond type offers unique benefits and risks, and a well-structured bond portfolio may include a mix of these bonds to achieve diversification and align with the investor's financial objectives.

The Role of Bonds in a Balanced Investment Portfolio

Bonds play a crucial role in a balanced investment portfolio by providing stability, income, and diversification. Including bonds alongside other asset classes, such as stocks, can help investors achieve their financial objectives while managing overall portfolio risk.

- **Stability and Capital Preservation**

- Lower Volatility: Bonds generally exhibit lower price volatility compared to stocks, providing stability during periods of market turbulence.
- Risk Mitigation: Including bonds can help mitigate the impact of stock market downturns on the overall portfolio.

- **Income Generation**
    - Regular Interest Payments: Bonds provide a predictable income stream through regular interest (coupon) payments, which can be especially attractive for income-seeking investors, retirees, or those looking to supplement their cash flow.
- **Diversification**

- Reducing Correlation: Bonds often have a lower correlation with stocks, meaning their price movements may not closely follow those of the stock market.
- Spreading Risk: Including bonds in a portfolio can reduce concentration risk associated with holding only one asset class, helping to spread risk across different investment types.

- **Risk Management**

- Matching Time Horizons: For investors with specific financial goals and timeframes, such as funding a child's education or retirement, bonds with appropriate maturities can align with those goals.
- Reducing Interest Rate Risk: By diversifying bond holdings with various maturities, investors can mitigate the impact of interest rate fluctuations on the portfolio's overall value.

- **Preservation of Capital During Retirement**
    - Capital Preservation: For retirees or those nearing

retirement, having a portion of the portfolio allocated to bonds can help preserve capital and maintain a stable income stream.

- **Rebalancing Tool**
    - Maintaining Target Allocation: As the stock market fluctuates, the portfolio's allocation may shift. Rebalancing involves selling or buying assets (such as bonds) to restore the desired asset allocation.
- **Different Types of Bonds**
    - Tailoring Risk-Return Profile: Investors can choose from various bond types, such as government bonds, corporate bonds, and municipal bonds, to tailor the portfolio's risk-return profile to their preferences.
- **Considerations**

- Risk Tolerance: Conservative investors may allocate a larger portion to bonds for stability, while more aggressive investors may have a higher allocation to stocks for growth potential.
- Investment Horizon: The time horizon for financial goals plays a role in determining the appropriate allocation to bonds.
- Economic Conditions: Inflation expectations and interest rate outlook can influence bond performance.

It's crucial for investors to carefully assess their risk tolerance, investment objectives, and time horizon when incorporating bonds into their portfolio. A balanced and diversified investment approach can help investors navigate market fluctuations and achieve long-term financial success while managing risk effectively. Regular portfolio review and adjustments may be necessary to maintain the desired asset allocation over time.

Chapter 4: Mutual Funds and Exchange-Traded Funds (ETFs)

What are Mutual Funds and ETFs and How They Operate

Mutual funds and exchange-traded funds (ETFs) are popular investment vehicles that pool money from multiple investors to invest in a diversified portfolio of securities. They provide individual investors with access to a wide range of assets and professional management, making investing more accessible and convenient.

- **Mutual Funds**

- Definition: Mutual funds are collective investment schemes managed by professional fund managers who pool money from multiple investors to invest in a diversified portfolio of stocks, bonds, or other securities.
- Ownership: When you invest in a mutual fund, you become a shareholder of the fund, and your ownership is represented by the number of fund shares you hold.
- Net Asset Value (NAV): The NAV represents the per-share value of the mutual fund and is calculated daily based on the current market value of the fund's assets minus its liabilities.

- **How Mutual Funds Operate**

- Professional Management: Mutual funds are managed by experienced investment professionals who make decisions about buying, selling, and holding the fund's underlying securities.
- Diversification: Mutual funds invest in a wide range of securities, which helps spread risk across various assets and

industries.

- Regulatory Oversight: Mutual funds are subject to regulatory oversight to protect investors' interests and ensure compliance with investment guidelines.

- **Types of Mutual Funds**

- Equity Funds: Invest primarily in stocks, aiming for capital appreciation.
- Bond Funds: Primarily invest in bonds, seeking income and stability.
- Balanced Funds: Invest in a mix of stocks and bonds to achieve a balance between growth and income.
- Index Funds: Mirror a specific market index's performance, aiming to replicate its returns.
- Sector Funds: Concentrate on a specific sector or industry, providing targeted exposure to particular segments of the market.
- Target-Date Funds: Adjust asset allocation based on the investor's target retirement date, becoming more conservative as the date approaches.

- **Exchange-Traded Funds (ETFs)**

- Definition: ETFs are similar to mutual funds in that they pool money from multiple investors to invest in a diversified portfolio of assets. However, unlike mutual funds, ETF shares trade on stock exchanges throughout the trading day, like individual stocks.
- Liquidity: ETFs offer high liquidity, as investors can buy and sell shares during market hours at real-time market prices.
- Intraday Trading: ETFs allow investors to trade throughout the trading session, enabling them to take advantage of price

fluctuations.

- **How ETFs Operate**

- Creation and Redemption: ETF shares are created or redeemed by authorized participants (large institutional investors) through an in-kind exchange process with the ETF provider. This process helps keep the ETF's share price closely aligned with the net asset value of its underlying assets.
- Tracking an Index: Many ETFs aim to replicate the performance of a specific market index, holding a similar composition of securities as the index.

- **Types of ETFs**

- Equity ETFs: Track stock market indices, providing exposure to various segments of the stock market.
- Bond ETFs: Focus on fixed-income securities, offering diversification across different types of bonds.
- Commodity ETFs: Invest in physical commodities like gold, silver, oil, or agricultural products.
- Currency ETFs: Provide exposure to foreign currencies relative to a base currency.

Mutual funds and ETFs provide investors with an efficient way to access a diverse range of investment opportunities without the need for individual stock or bond selection. They offer simplicity, professional management, and liquidity, making them suitable for investors of all experience levels and financial goals. Understanding the differences between mutual funds and ETFs and how they operate can help investors choose the most suitable investment option for their specific needs.

Understanding the Benefits of Diversification

Diversification is a fundamental investment strategy that involves spreading investments across different assets, industries, regions, or investment types. It is an essential approach for managing risk and achieving more stable returns in a portfolio. Both mutual funds and ETFs can help investors achieve diversification effectively. Here are the key benefits of diversification:

- **Risk Reduction**

- Spreading Risk: Diversification helps reduce the impact of individual asset volatility on the overall portfolio. When some assets decline in value, others may rise or remain stable, mitigating the negative impact.
- Asset Class Diversification: Investing in various asset classes, such as stocks, bonds, and cash, ensures that your portfolio isn't solely dependent on the performance of a single asset type.

- **Stable Returns**

- Smoothing Returns: Diversification can lead to more consistent returns over time, as the positive performance of some assets can help offset the negative performance of others.
- Lower Portfolio Volatility: A well-diversified portfolio typically experiences less extreme fluctuations, providing investors with a smoother ride in the market.

- **Protection Against Market Events**

- Market Cycles: Different assets tend to perform better during various economic and market cycles. Diversification can help protect your portfolio from severe losses during market downturns or economic recessions.

- Unpredictable Events: Unexpected events, such as geopolitical events or industry-specific disruptions, can significantly impact individual assets. Diversification can reduce the risk of a single event having a disproportionately negative effect on your portfolio.

- **Opportunity to Capture Growth**

- Potential for Growth: Diversification allows you to participate in the growth potential of different assets and industries, even if some individual investments may underperform.
- Risk and Reward Balance: By combining assets with varying levels of risk and return potential, diversification helps strike a balance between potential growth and risk management.

- **Psychological Benefits**

- Reducing Emotional Decisions: Diversification can help reduce emotional decision-making driven by short-term market movements, as the overall portfolio impact may be less dramatic.
- Long-Term Focus: A well-diversified portfolio encourages a long-term investment perspective, reducing the temptation to make impulsive changes in response to short-term market fluctuations.

- **Convenience and Cost-Effectiveness**

- Mutual Funds and ETFs: Investing in mutual funds and ETFs

automatically provides diversification within a single investment vehicle, reducing the need for individual stock or bond selection.
- Lower Transaction Costs: Owning a diversified portfolio through funds can be more cost-effective than directly purchasing multiple individual assets.

Diversification is a powerful risk management tool that allows investors to take advantage of various investment opportunities while reducing the impact of negative market events. By spreading investments across multiple assets, investors can achieve a more stable and resilient portfolio capable of weathering different market conditions. Mutual funds and ETFs are excellent choices for diversification, as they offer access to a wide range of assets and professional management, making diversification more accessible and convenient for individual investors.

How to Choose the Right Mutual Funds and ETFs for Your Investment Goals

Selecting the appropriate mutual funds and ETFs is crucial for aligning your investment strategy with your financial objectives and risk tolerance. Here are essential steps to help you make informed decisions:

- **Clarify Your Investment Goals**

- Define Objectives: Determine your investment goals, such as long-term growth, current income, capital preservation, or a combination of these.
- Time Horizon: Assess the time you can stay invested to achieve your goals. Longer investment horizons may allow for more aggressive strategies.

- **Risk Tolerance**

    - Evaluate Risk Tolerance: Understand how comfortable you are with fluctuations in your portfolio's value. Higher-risk assets may offer greater potential returns but come with increased volatility.
- **Asset Allocation**
    - Balancing Asset Classes: Decide on the proportion of stocks, bonds, and other assets you want in your portfolio. Asset allocation is a key factor influencing overall portfolio performance.
- **Expense Ratios and Fees**
    - Compare Costs: Consider expense ratios and management fees associated with mutual funds and ETFs. Lower costs can enhance long-term returns.
- **Historical Performance**
    - Past Performance: Review the historical performance of the funds over different timeframes. However, remember that past performance does not guarantee future results.
- **Fund Manager and Company Reputation**

- Fund Manager Experience: Look into the fund manager's experience and track record. Experienced and skilled managers may contribute to the fund's success.
- Fund Company Reputation: Assess the reputation and stability of the fund company. Established and reputable firms often provide more reliable services.

- **Diversification and Holdings**
    - Portfolio Holdings: Analyze the fund's holdings to ensure they align with your investment objectives. Check if the fund's diversification matches your desired asset allocation.

- **Risk Measures**
    - Risk Metrics: Evaluate risk measures such as standard deviation and beta to understand the fund's historical volatility and sensitivity to market movements.
- **Benchmark Comparison**
    - Compare to Benchmark: Assess how the fund's performance compares to its benchmark index. This helps determine if the fund's returns are on par with its stated objective.
- **Tax Efficiency (for taxable accounts)**
    - Tax Considerations: In taxable accounts, consider tax-efficient funds or ETFs that aim to minimize capital gains distributions.
- **Read the Prospectus**
    - Fund Prospectus: Carefully read the fund's prospectus, which provides essential information about its investment strategy, risks, fees, and performance.
- **Consider Professional Advice**
    - Financial Advisor: If you are unsure about fund selection or your investment strategy, seek advice from a qualified financial advisor who can provide personalized recommendations.

Remember that each individual's investment needs are unique, and there is no one-size-fits-all approach to choosing mutual funds and ETFs. A well-diversified portfolio typically includes a mix of assets that align with your financial goals and risk tolerance. Regularly review your portfolio to ensure it remains aligned with your changing circumstances and investment objectives.

The Impact of Expense Ratios on Your Returns

Expense ratios are a crucial factor to consider when investing in mutual funds and ETFs, as they directly impact your overall returns over time. Understanding the impact of expense ratios is essential for optimizing the cost-effectiveness of your investment portfolio. Here's how expense ratios influence your returns:

- **What are Expense Ratios?**

- Expense ratios represent the annual fees charged by mutual funds and ETFs to cover their operating expenses. They are expressed as a percentage of the fund's total assets under management (AUM).
- These fees include fund management expenses, administrative costs, marketing fees, and other operational charges incurred by the fund.

- **Reducing Your Investment Returns**

- Compounding Effect: Over time, expense ratios can significantly reduce the compounding growth of your investments.
- Lower Net Returns: As expense ratios are deducted from the fund's assets, your returns will be lower than the fund's gross returns.

- **Example of the Impact**

Time Horizon	Gross Return (7%)	Expense Ratio (1%)	Net Return
1 year	$700	$100	$600
5 years	$4,081	$585	$3,496
10 years	$19,672	$2,836	$16,836
20 years	$76,122	$14,663	$61,459

- Let's say you invest $10,000 in a mutual fund or ETF with an expense ratio of 1%. Assuming the fund's gross annual return is 7%, here's how the expense ratio affects your returns over different time horizons:
- As illustrated above, over time, the compounding effect of the expense ratio becomes more pronounced, leading to a significant difference in net returns compared to the fund's gross returns.

- **Importance of Low Expense Ratios**

- Minimizing Costs: Choosing funds with lower expense ratios can significantly reduce the impact of fees on your overall returns.
- Consistent Advantage: Over the long term, funds with lower expense ratios tend to outperform higher-cost funds.

- **Comparing Expense Ratios**

- Benchmarking: When evaluating funds, compare their expense ratios to similar funds within the same asset class and investment style.
- Cost-Effective Choices: Generally, index funds and ETFs tend to have lower expense ratios compared to actively managed funds.

- **Tax Efficiency**
    - Tax Considerations: Lower expense ratios can also contribute to greater tax efficiency in taxable accounts, as capital gains distributions are minimized.
- **Balancing Costs and Performance**

- Performance Matters: While expense ratios are essential, investors should also consider the fund's historical performance, investment strategy, and risk-adjusted returns.
- Total Return Approach: Focus on the fund's total return (capital appreciation plus income) after accounting for the expense ratio.

By choosing funds with lower expense ratios, investors can maximize their long-term investment returns. Reducing fees is one of the few factors within an investor's control, making it a crucial aspect of successful portfolio management. However, remember that expense ratios are not the only consideration; a well-rounded evaluation of the fund's strategy, performance, and risk characteristics is necessary for making informed investment decisions.

Chapter 5: Building Your Investment Strategy

Assessing Your Risk Tolerance and Investment Goals

Before constructing your investment strategy, it's essential to assess your risk tolerance and clearly define your investment goals. Understanding your comfort level with risk and your financial objectives will help shape a portfolio that aligns with your needs. Here are the key steps:

- **Risk Tolerance**

- Emotional Comfort: Evaluate how comfortable you are with the possibility of your investments experiencing fluctuations in value. Consider your ability to stay invested during market downturns without making impulsive decisions.
- Risk Capacity: Assess your financial capacity to take on risk. Factors such as income stability, age, financial obligations, and other investments impact your ability to handle risk.

- **Investment Goals**

- Short-Term vs. Long-Term Goals: Differentiate between short-term objectives, such as buying a house or funding a vacation, and long-term goals, like retirement or financial independence.
- Time Horizon: Determine the timeframe within which you need to achieve your goals. Longer investment horizons may allow for more aggressive investment strategies.

- **Return Expectations**

- Realistic Expectations: Set realistic expectations for the returns you anticipate from your investments. Understand that higher returns usually come with higher risk.
- Aligning with Goals: Ensure that your return expectations align with the growth needed to achieve your investment objectives.

- **Financial Situation**

- Current Financial Position: Assess your current financial situation, including income, expenses, debt levels, and existing assets.
- Emergency Fund: Before investing, establish an emergency fund to cover unexpected expenses, ensuring that your investments remain intact during emergencies.

- **Diversification**

- Balancing Risk and Return: Determine the appropriate asset allocation (e.g., stocks, bonds, cash) that matches your risk tolerance and investment goals.
- Geographic and Industry Diversification: Consider diversifying across different geographic regions and industries to spread risk further.

- **Investment Timeframe and Liquidity Needs**

- Time-Sensitive Goals: Evaluate the liquidity needs of your investments. Short-term goals may require more liquid and stable assets to access funds quickly.
- Lock-In Periods: Be aware of any investments with lock-in periods or penalties for early withdrawals.

- **Inflation and Taxes**

- Inflation Impact: Consider the impact of inflation on your investments' purchasing power over time. Some investments, like stocks, historically provide better protection against inflation.
- Tax Implications: Understand the tax implications of your investments, especially in taxable accounts. Tax-efficient strategies can help maximize after-tax returns.

- **Regular Review and Adjustments**
    - Dynamic Process: Recognize that your risk tolerance and investment goals may change over time due to life events or shifting economic conditions. Regularly review and adjust your investment strategy accordingly.
- **Seeking Professional Advice**
    - Financial Advisor: If you're uncertain about your risk tolerance, investment goals, or portfolio construction, seek guidance from a qualified financial advisor who can provide personalized recommendations.

Assessing your risk tolerance and investment goals is a foundational step in building a well-structured investment strategy. A clear understanding of your financial situation, risk capacity, and time horizons will guide your asset allocation decisions and help you create a diversified portfolio that aligns with your long-term objectives. Regularly revisiting and fine-tuning your investment strategy will ensure it remains in sync with your changing circumstances and evolving financial aspirations.

The Importance of Asset Allocation in Your Portfolio

Asset allocation is one of the most critical factors influencing investment success. It refers to the strategic distribution of your investment capital across different asset classes, such as stocks, bonds, cash, and alternative investments. Here's why asset allocation is essential for your portfolio:

- **Risk Management**

- Diversification: Asset allocation involves spreading your investments across various asset classes and securities. Diversification helps reduce the impact of individual asset risk on the overall portfolio, enhancing risk management.
- Balancing Risk and Return: By combining assets with varying risk levels, you can tailor your portfolio to match your risk tolerance and investment goals.

- **Enhanced Returns**

- Capitalizing on Growth Opportunities: Allocating a portion of your portfolio to growth-oriented assets like stocks allows you to capitalize on their potential for long-term appreciation and wealth accumulation.
- Stability through Bonds: Including bonds and other fixed-income assets in your allocation can provide stability and steady income, especially during periods of stock market volatility.

- **Matching Investment Goals**
    - Alignment with Objectives: Asset allocation allows you to tailor your portfolio to match your specific investment goals and time horizons. It ensures that your investments are working in harmony with your financial aspirations.

- **Managing Market Volatility**

- Reducing Portfolio Fluctuations: A well-structured asset allocation can help cushion the impact of market downturns and reduce the overall volatility of your portfolio.
- Avoiding Overreliance on One Asset: Over-concentration in a single asset class increases vulnerability to adverse market movements.

- **Long-Term Perspective**

- Patience and Discipline: Asset allocation encourages a long-term investment perspective, promoting patience and discipline during market fluctuations.
- Avoiding Emotional Decisions: A balanced portfolio reduces the temptation to make hasty decisions based on short-term market movements.

- **Flexibility and Adjustments**

- Life Changes: Asset allocation allows you to adjust your portfolio as your financial situation and goals change over time. It's adaptable to accommodate new life events and priorities.
- Rebalancing: Regularly rebalancing your portfolio ensures that it remains aligned with your target asset allocation, maintaining your desired risk-return profile.

- **Customization for Individuals**

- Personalized Approach: Asset allocation can be customized to suit an individual's unique risk tolerance, investment goals, and financial situation.

- Suitability for All Investors: Whether you are a conservative or aggressive investor, asset allocation can be tailored to meet your needs.

- **Research-Backed Strategy**
    - Investment Research: Asset allocation is supported by decades of academic research, which has consistently demonstrated its significance in determining portfolio performance.

In summary, asset allocation is a fundamental tool for creating a well-structured and diversified investment portfolio. It plays a crucial role in managing risk, maximizing returns, and aligning your investments with your long-term financial goals. Regularly reviewing and adjusting your asset allocation ensures that your portfolio remains on track to achieve your objectives, even as market conditions and your personal circumstances evolve.

Long-Term vs. Short-Term Investing Strategies

When developing your investment strategy, it's essential to consider the differences between long-term and short-term investing approaches. Each strategy has its advantages and aligns with specific investment goals and risk tolerances.

- **Long-Term Investing**

- Time Horizon: Long-term investing involves holding investments for an extended period, typically several years or even decades.
- Focus on Fundamentals: Long-term investors prioritize the underlying fundamentals of their investments, such as company performance, earnings growth, and economic trends.

- Riding Market Cycles: Long-term investors are more willing to weather market fluctuations, knowing that markets tend to recover over extended periods.
- Patience and Discipline: This approach requires patience and discipline, as the investor remains committed to their strategy despite short-term market turbulence.
- Advantages:

- Power of Compounding: Long-term investors benefit from the compounding effect, where their returns generate additional returns over time.
- Reduced Transaction Costs: Fewer frequent trades result in lower transaction costs, enhancing overall portfolio returns.
- Lower Taxation: Long-term capital gains tax rates are typically more favorable than short-term capital gains tax rates.

- **Short-Term Investing (Trading)**

- Time Horizon: Short-term investing, also known as trading, involves holding investments for a brief period, often days, weeks, or a few months.
- Focus on Price Movements: Traders focus on technical analysis and short-term price movements to identify entry and exit points for quick profits.
- Capitalizing on Volatility: Short-term investors aim to profit from short-term market movements and volatility, buying low and selling high within a shorter timeframe.
- Active Management: Trading requires constant monitoring of the market and frequent trading decisions.
- Advantages:

- Potential Quick Gains: Successful short-term trades can lead to quick profits, which may be appealing to some investors.

- Flexibility: Short-term investors have the flexibility to quickly respond to changing market conditions and adapt their strategies accordingly.

- **Finding the Right Approach**

- Aligning with Goals: The choice between long-term and short-term strategies depends on your investment goals, risk tolerance, and time horizon.
- Diversification: Investors may choose a combination of both strategies to balance long-term growth with potential short-term opportunities.
- Matching Personality: The chosen approach should also align with your personality, investment knowledge, and comfort level with risk.

- **Importance of Staying Consistent**

- Avoid Timing the Market: Trying to time the market by switching between short-term and long-term strategies based on market conditions can lead to suboptimal results.
- Staying Disciplined: Regardless of the chosen strategy, consistency and discipline are key to successful investing.

- **Long-Term and Short-Term Instruments**

- Long-Term: Investing in individual stocks, bonds, mutual funds, and ETFs can be suitable for long-term strategies.
- Short-Term: Short-term strategies may involve day trading, swing trading, or using derivatives like options and futures.

Ultimately, the decision between long-term and short-term investing strategies depends on your investment objectives, risk tolerance, and time horizon. Both approaches have their merits and can be valuable components of an overall investment plan. Building a well-diversified portfolio that aligns with your financial goals and risk tolerance is crucial for achieving success, regardless of your chosen investment strategy.

Dollar-Cost Averaging and Its Advantages

Dollar-cost averaging (DCA) is an investment strategy that involves investing a fixed amount of money at regular intervals, regardless of market conditions. This approach has several advantages, making it a popular choice for long-term investors:

- **Risk Mitigation**

- Smoothing Market Volatility: DCA helps mitigate the impact of market volatility on your investments. By investing consistently over time, you buy more shares when prices are low and fewer shares when prices are high, effectively lowering your average cost per share.
- Avoiding Market Timing: DCA removes the need to time the market, as investments are made at regular intervals. This reduces the risk of making poor investment decisions based on short-term market fluctuations.

- **Disciplined Approach**

- Encourages Consistency: DCA encourages disciplined investing, as you commit to investing a fixed amount regularly, regardless of market sentiment.
- Reducing Emotional Decisions: Emotional reactions to market swings may lead to impulsive investment decisions.

DCA helps investors stay focused on their long-term goals.

- **Automatic Investing**

- Convenient and Easy: DCA is relatively easy to implement, making it accessible to both experienced and novice investors.
- Automatic Contributions: Many investment platforms allow automatic contributions, making it a hands-off approach for investors who want to build wealth gradually.

- **Long-Term Benefits**

- Capitalizing on Market Downturns: DCA allows investors to take advantage of market downturns by purchasing more shares at lower prices, potentially positioning them for higher returns when markets recover.
- Dollar-Cost Averaging Effect: Over time, DCA's averaged cost per share may be lower than the average share price, contributing to potential overall gains.

- **Consistent Investment Habit**

- Building Good Financial Habits: DCA cultivates a consistent investment habit, which can be beneficial for financial planning and achieving long-term goals.
- Reducing Timing Anxiety: Investors are less likely to worry about the perfect timing to invest when they have a predetermined investment schedule.

- **Applicability to Volatile Assets**
    - Suitable for Volatile Markets: DCA is particularly useful for investing in volatile assets like stocks or cryptocurrencies, where prices can experience

significant fluctuations.

- **Lowering Overall Risk**

- Diversification of Purchase Prices: Through DCA, investments are made at various price levels, leading to a diversified entry point into the market.
- Reducing Potential Regret: If an investor's initial investment declines significantly soon after entering the market, DCA can help reduce feelings of regret.

- **Gradual Market Participation**
    - Smoothing Lump-Sum Risk: For investors with a large sum of money to invest, DCA can smooth the risk of entering the market all at once, especially if timing the market is uncertain.

While dollar-cost averaging offers several advantages, it's essential to recognize that no investment strategy guarantees profits or eliminates all risks. DCA is most effective when used as a long-term strategy, as its benefits are more pronounced over extended investment periods. By embracing disciplined and consistent investing, investors can potentially build wealth over time and work toward achieving their financial goals.

Chapter 6: Market Analysis and Investment Research

Fundamentals vs. Technical Analysis

When analyzing investment opportunities, investors can use two primary methods: fundamentals analysis and technical analysis. Each approach offers different perspectives on how to evaluate assets and make investment decisions.

- **Fundamentals Analysis**

- Understanding the Business: Fundamentals analysis involves studying the underlying factors of an investment, such as a company's financial health, business model, management team, and competitive advantages.
- Focus on Intrinsic Value: The goal of fundamentals analysis is to assess whether an asset is undervalued or overvalued based on its intrinsic value. Investors look for assets that may have a higher intrinsic value than their current market price, indicating a potential buying opportunity.
- Key Metrics: Fundamental analysts examine financial statements, earnings reports, revenue growth, profit margins, and other key metrics to gain insights into a company's financial performance.
- Long-Term Perspective: Fundamentals analysis is often associated with long-term investing, as it aims to identify assets with solid fundamentals that can generate value over time.
- Commonly Used for: Stocks, bonds, real estate, and other assets where underlying financial data is crucial in determining value.

- **Technical Analysis**

- Price and Volume Trends: Technical analysis focuses on studying historical price and volume data of an asset to identify patterns and trends that can help predict future price movements.
- Chart Patterns: Technical analysts use various chart patterns, such as support and resistance levels, moving averages, and trend lines, to identify potential entry and exit points for trades.
- Market Psychology: Technical analysis assumes that market participants' behaviors are reflected in the price movements of assets. Patterns and trends can indicate investor sentiment and market psychology.
- Short-Term Perspective: Technical analysis is often associated with short-term trading and making tactical decisions based on short-term price movements.
- Commonly Used for: Stocks, currencies, commodities, and other assets with liquid and actively traded markets.

- **Combining Both Approaches**

- Some investors use a combination of fundamentals and technical analysis to make investment decisions. This approach is known as "fusion analysis" and aims to benefit from the strengths of both methods.
- Fundamental analysis can provide the "what to buy" perspective, identifying undervalued assets with solid long-term potential.
- Technical analysis can provide the "when to buy" or "when to sell" perspective, helping investors time their trades and optimize entry and exit points.

- **Importance of Due Diligence**

- Regardless of the analysis method used, conducting thorough due diligence is essential. Investors should research and understand the assets they plan to invest in, their risk factors, and potential growth prospects.
- No Guarantees: It's essential to recognize that both fundamental and technical analysis have limitations, and no approach guarantees investment success. Market conditions and unexpected events can impact asset performance.

- **Investment Horizon and Objectives**

- The choice between fundamentals and technical analysis may depend on an investor's investment horizon, risk tolerance, and financial objectives.
- Long-term investors focused on buying quality assets may lean more toward fundamentals analysis, while short-term traders aiming to profit from price movements may favor technical analysis.

By understanding both fundamentals and technical analysis, investors can make more informed decisions and build a well-rounded investment strategy. Each approach offers unique insights into market behavior, and combining them can provide a comprehensive view of potential investment opportunities. It's crucial for investors to align their analysis method with their investment goals and risk tolerance for the most effective decision-making process.

Key Financial Metrics to Evaluate Stocks and Companies

When analyzing stocks and companies, investors rely on several key financial metrics to assess their financial health, performance, and potential for growth. Understanding these metrics can help investors make informed decisions and identify investment opportunities. Here are some essential financial metrics to consider:

- **Earnings per Share (EPS)**

- Definition: EPS represents a company's profitability on a per-share basis. It is calculated by dividing the company's net earnings by the number of outstanding shares.
- Significance: Higher EPS generally indicates greater profitability and a company's ability to generate earnings for its shareholders.

- **Price-to-Earnings Ratio (P/E Ratio)**

- Definition: The P/E ratio compares a company's stock price to its earnings per share. It is calculated by dividing the current stock price by the EPS.
- Significance: The P/E ratio helps investors understand how much they are paying for each dollar of the company's earnings. A higher P/E ratio suggests a higher valuation relative to earnings.

- **Dividend Yield**

- Definition: Dividend yield is the annual dividend per share divided by the current stock price, expressed as a percentage.
- Significance: Dividend yield indicates the income a shareholder can expect to receive from holding the stock. It is particularly relevant for income-focused investors.

- **Return on Equity (ROE)**

- Definition: ROE measures a company's profitability relative to shareholders' equity. It is calculated by dividing net income by shareholders' equity.

- Significance: ROE provides insights into how effectively a company utilizes shareholders' investments to generate profits.

- **Debt-to-Equity Ratio (D/E Ratio)**

- Definition: The D/E ratio compares a company's total debt to its shareholders' equity. It is calculated by dividing total debt by shareholders' equity.
- Significance: The D/E ratio assesses a company's financial leverage. A high D/E ratio may indicate higher financial risk.

- **Gross Margin**

- Definition: Gross margin represents the percentage of revenue that exceeds the cost of goods sold (COGS). It is calculated by subtracting COGS from total revenue and dividing the result by total revenue.
- Significance: Gross margin measures a company's ability to control production costs and pricing power.

- **Operating Margin**

- Definition: Operating margin measures a company's operating efficiency by comparing operating income to total revenue. It is calculated by dividing operating income by total revenue.
- Significance: Operating margin indicates how much profit a company generates from its core business operations.

- **Free Cash Flow (FCF)**

- Definition: FCF represents the cash generated by a company after accounting for capital expenditures and operating expenses.
- Significance: FCF is a critical metric to assess a company's financial health and ability to invest in growth opportunities, pay dividends, or reduce debt.

- **Current Ratio**

- Definition: The current ratio evaluates a company's liquidity by dividing its current assets by its current liabilities.
- Significance: A current ratio above 1 indicates that a company has sufficient current assets to cover its short-term liabilities.

- **Price-to-Book Ratio (P/B Ratio)**

- Definition: The P/B ratio compares a company's stock price to its book value per share. It is calculated by dividing the current stock price by the book value per share.
- Significance: The P/B ratio helps investors understand how the market values a company's assets relative to its share price.

By analyzing these key financial metrics, investors can gain valuable insights into a company's financial health, profitability, and growth prospects. However, it's essential to use these metrics in conjunction with other qualitative and quantitative factors to make well-rounded investment decisions. Additionally, comparing these metrics to industry peers and historical data can provide context for better assessments of a company's performance.

Analyzing Macroeconomic Factors and Their Impact on the Market

Macroeconomic factors refer to broader economic conditions and trends that can influence the overall performance of financial markets. Understanding these factors can help investors make informed decisions and navigate market conditions. Here are some key macroeconomic factors and their impact on the market:

- **Economic Growth (GDP)**
    - Impact: Economic growth, as measured by Gross Domestic Product (GDP), affects investor sentiment and market performance. Strong GDP growth is generally associated with a bullish market, while weak or negative growth may lead to a bearish market.
- **Interest Rates**
    - Impact: Central banks set interest rates, and changes in rates can significantly impact various asset classes. Lower interest rates generally stimulate borrowing, spending, and investment, benefiting stocks and other riskier assets. Conversely, higher rates may lead to a shift towards more conservative investments.
- **Inflation**
    - Impact: Inflation, the rate at which the general price level rises, can erode the purchasing power of money. Moderate inflation is generally positive for markets, but high inflation can lead to uncertainty and market volatility.
- **Employment and Unemployment**
    - Impact: Labor market conditions influence consumer spending, corporate profitability, and overall economic health. Low unemployment rates are generally positive for markets, while high unemployment can signal economic weakness.

- **Consumer Spending**
    - Impact: Consumer spending is a critical driver of economic growth, as it accounts for a significant portion of GDP. Strong consumer spending is favorable for companies, especially those in consumer-oriented sectors.
- **Business Investment**
    - Impact: Business investment reflects companies' confidence in the economy. Increased business investment can lead to job creation, innovation, and overall economic growth.
- **Trade and Current Account Balances**
    - Impact: Trade balances, reflecting the difference between a country's exports and imports, can influence currency values and international trade relations. Trade deficits or surpluses can impact market sentiment.
- **Geopolitical Events**
    - Impact: Political instability, international conflicts, and geopolitical events can lead to market uncertainty and volatility. Investors may become more risk-averse during periods of heightened geopolitical tension.
- **Monetary Policy**
    - Impact: Decisions made by central banks regarding interest rates and money supply can directly impact financial markets and the cost of borrowing.
- **Fiscal Policy**
    - Impact: Government spending and taxation policies can influence economic growth, consumer behavior, and corporate performance, which in turn affect financial markets.

- **Global Economic Conditions**
    - Impact: Global economic trends and conditions can have spill-over effects on domestic markets, especially in an interconnected world economy.
- **Technological Advancements**
    - Impact: Technological innovations can disrupt industries and create new investment opportunities, driving market performance.

Investors should closely monitor these macroeconomic factors and consider their potential impact on specific assets and sectors. While macroeconomic analysis is valuable, it is essential to also assess microeconomic factors, such as individual company performance and industry-specific trends, to gain a comprehensive view of the investment landscape. Additionally, unforeseen events and external shocks can influence markets, highlighting the importance of staying informed and adaptable as an investor.

Utilizing Online Resources for Investment Research

The internet has revolutionized the way investors access information and conduct investment research. There is a wealth of online resources available that can provide valuable insights, data, and analysis to aid in making informed investment decisions. Here are some key online resources that investors can leverage for their research:

- **Financial News Websites**

- Financial news websites like Bloomberg, Reuters, CNBC, and Yahoo Finance offer up-to-date news, market analysis, and economic updates.
- Investors can stay informed about market-moving events, corporate earnings releases, and economic indicators that

may impact their investments.

- **Company Websites and Investor Relations**

- Company websites and investor relations pages provide official corporate information, financial reports, and presentations.
- Investors can access quarterly earnings reports, annual reports, and other essential financial data directly from the source.

- **Financial Statements and Filings**

- Websites like the U.S. Securities and Exchange Commission's EDGAR database allow investors to access public companies' financial statements and regulatory filings.
- Analyzing financial statements helps investors evaluate a company's performance, profitability, and financial health.

- **Stock Screeners**

- Stock screeners on platforms like Yahoo Finance and Google Finance allow investors to filter stocks based on various criteria such as price, market cap, dividend yield, and financial ratios.
- Screeners help investors identify potential investment opportunities that meet specific criteria.

- **Analyst Reports**

- Online brokerage platforms and financial websites often provide analyst reports from reputable research firms.
- Analyst reports offer insights into a company's prospects,

target price, and investment recommendations.

- **Investment Forums and Social Media**

- Online investment forums like Reddit's r/investing and social media platforms like Twitter can provide valuable insights from a community of investors.
- However, investors should exercise caution and critically evaluate information from these sources, as not all content may be accurate or reliable.

- **Financial Blogs and Educational Websites**

- Financial blogs and educational websites offer valuable articles, tutorials, and research on various investment topics.
- Investors can expand their knowledge and stay updated on market trends and investment strategies.

- **Economic Data and Research**

- Websites like the World Bank, Federal Reserve, and the Bureau of Economic Analysis provide economic data and research reports.
- Investors can access macroeconomic indicators and reports that influence investment decisions.

- **Online Brokerage Platforms**

- Online brokerage platforms often offer research tools, market analysis, and educational resources to their customers.
- Investors can access real-time quotes, charts, and financial news on these platforms.

- **Financial Data Aggregators**

- Financial data aggregators like Morningstar and FactSet compile comprehensive financial data and analysis on various investment products.
- Investors can access fund performance, expense ratios, and holdings data for mutual funds and ETFs.

By utilizing these online resources, investors can access a vast amount of information and analysis to support their investment decisions. However, it's crucial to verify the credibility of sources, cross-reference information, and conduct due diligence before making any investment choices. Combining online research with an understanding of fundamental and technical analysis can enhance the quality of investment decisions and support long-term financial goals.

Chapter 7: Investing in a Tax-Efficient Way

Understanding the Tax Implications of Different Investments

Investing in a tax-efficient manner is crucial for maximizing after-tax returns and preserving wealth. Different types of investments have varying tax implications, and understanding these implications can help investors make tax-smart decisions. Here are some key points to consider:

- **Taxable vs. Tax-Advantaged Accounts**

- Taxable Accounts: Investments held in taxable brokerage accounts are subject to taxation on dividends, capital gains, and interest income. It's essential to be aware of the tax consequences of buying, selling, or receiving income from these investments.
- Tax-Advantaged Accounts: Accounts like Individual Retirement Accounts (IRAs) and 401(k)s offer tax benefits, such as tax-deferred growth or tax-free withdrawals in retirement. Utilizing these accounts can significantly reduce the tax burden on your investments.

- **Capital Gains Taxes**

- Short-Term vs. Long-Term: In most countries, capital gains on investments held for one year or less are considered short-term and taxed at a higher rate than gains on investments held for more than one year, which are considered long-term and usually taxed at a lower rate.
- Harvesting Losses: Investors can strategically sell investments

at a loss to offset capital gains and potentially reduce their overall tax liability. This practice is known as tax-loss harvesting.

- **Dividend Taxes**

- Qualified vs. Non-Qualified: Dividends from qualified sources may be eligible for lower tax rates, while non-qualified dividends are taxed at the individual's ordinary income tax rate.
- Dividend Reinvestment Plans (DRIPs): Reinvested dividends may still be taxable in the year they are received, even if they are not distributed as cash.

- **Interest Income Taxes**

- Taxable Bonds: Interest income from taxable bonds is typically taxed at the individual's ordinary income tax rate.
- Municipal Bonds: Interest income from municipal bonds issued by state or local governments may be tax-free at the federal level and potentially tax-free at the state level for residents of the issuing state.

- **Tax-Efficient Investments**

- Index Funds and ETFs: Passive investment vehicles like index funds and exchange-traded funds (ETFs) tend to have lower portfolio turnover, leading to fewer taxable events.
- Tax-Managed Funds: Some mutual funds are structured to minimize taxable distributions, making them more tax-efficient.

- **Asset Location**

- Placing tax-efficient investments in taxable accounts and tax-inefficient investments in tax-advantaged accounts can optimize tax outcomes.
- Tax-Efficient Asset Placement: Generally, tax-efficient investments like broad-market index funds may be better suited for taxable accounts, while tax-inefficient investments like actively managed funds may be more suitable for tax-advantaged accounts.

- **Qualified Dividends and Capital Gains**
    - In some countries, qualified dividends and long-term capital gains may be subject to lower tax rates than other forms of income, making them attractive investment options.
- **Roth vs. Traditional Retirement Accounts**

- Contributions to traditional retirement accounts (e.g., traditional IRAs, 401(k)s) may be tax-deductible in the year they are made, but withdrawals in retirement are taxed as ordinary income.
- Roth retirement accounts (e.g., Roth IRAs, Roth 401(k)s) are funded with after-tax contributions, but qualified withdrawals are generally tax-free.

- **Tax Considerations for Trading**

- Frequent trading in taxable accounts may trigger higher capital gains taxes and impact overall returns.
- Long-term buy-and-hold strategies can be more tax-efficient, as they reduce the frequency of taxable events.

Navigating the tax implications of investments can be complex, and it's advisable to consult with a tax advisor or financial professional to develop a tax-efficient investment strategy tailored to your specific financial situation and goals. Being mindful of taxes when making investment decisions can help investors preserve more of their wealth and achieve better long-term outcomes.

Strategies for Tax-Efficient Investing, such as Using Retirement Accounts

Investors can employ various strategies to optimize their investment approach and minimize tax liabilities. Utilizing retirement accounts is one of the most effective ways to achieve tax-efficient investing. Here are some strategies to consider:

- **Maximizing Contributions to Retirement Accounts**

- Contributions to tax-advantaged retirement accounts, such as Traditional IRAs, Roth IRAs, 401(k)s, and 403(b)s, offer tax benefits that can significantly impact long-term wealth accumulation.
- Traditional IRAs and 401(k)s allow for tax-deductible contributions, reducing taxable income in the year contributions are made.
- Roth IRAs and Roth 401(k)s use after-tax contributions, allowing for tax-free withdrawals in retirement.

- **Employer-Sponsored Retirement Plans**

- Many employers offer matching contributions to retirement plans, such as 401(k)s. Taking advantage of employer matches effectively provides "free money" and boosts retirement savings.
- Contributing to employer-sponsored plans not only reduces taxable income but also benefits from tax-deferred or tax-free growth, depending on the plan type.

- **Asset Location Optimization**

- Placing tax-efficient investments in taxable accounts and tax-inefficient investments in tax-advantaged accounts can improve after-tax returns.
- Tax-efficient investments, such as index funds and ETFs, may be better suited for taxable brokerage accounts, while actively managed funds or higher-yield assets may be placed in tax-advantaged retirement accounts.

- **Tax-Loss Harvesting**

- Tax-loss harvesting involves strategically selling investments at a loss to offset capital gains and potentially reduce overall tax liability.
- By realizing losses, investors can use them to offset capital gains or even deduct up to a certain amount against ordinary income.

- **Avoiding Short-Term Capital Gains**

- Holding investments for more than one year allows investors to benefit from lower long-term capital gains tax rates rather than higher short-term rates.
- Long-term buy-and-hold strategies can help investors avoid frequent short-term capital gains taxes.

- **Dividend Reinvestment Plans (DRIPs)**
    - In taxable accounts, investors should consider choosing to receive dividends in cash rather than reinvesting them. This approach can reduce taxable income and control tax liabilities.
- **Tax-Efficient Investment Vehicles**

    - Utilizing tax-efficient investment options, such as index funds and ETFs, can minimize capital gains distributions and taxable events.
- **Charitable Giving**
    - Donating appreciated assets to charity can be a tax-efficient way to reduce capital gains taxes. The donor may also receive a charitable deduction for the gift.
- **Avoiding High-Tax Investments in Taxable Accounts**
    - High-yield bonds or other investments generating significant interest income may be more suitable for tax-advantaged retirement accounts to avoid high taxes on interest earnings.
- **Tax-Aware Rebalancing**
    - When rebalancing a portfolio, consider doing so in a tax-efficient manner. Prioritize rebalancing within tax-advantaged accounts, where transactions do not trigger immediate taxable events.

It's important to note that tax laws and regulations vary between countries and can change over time. Investors should regularly review their investment strategies and tax planning with qualified tax advisors or financial professionals to ensure they remain aligned with their financial goals and the latest tax rules. By integrating tax-efficient strategies and utilizing retirement accounts effectively, investors can enhance their wealth accumulation and optimize their financial journey for the long term.

The Concept of Tax-Loss Harvesting

Tax-loss harvesting is a tax-efficient investment strategy that involves strategically selling investments that have experienced a loss to offset capital gains and potentially reduce the overall tax liability. This technique is often employed near the end of the tax year and can be an effective way to optimize after-tax returns. Here's how tax-loss harvesting works:

- **Identifying Losses**
    - Investors review their investment portfolio to identify securities that have declined in value since purchase. These are considered "realized losses" because they only become losses when the investment is sold.
- **Offsetting Capital Gains**

- If an investor has realized capital gains from other investments within the same tax year, tax-loss harvesting can be used to offset those gains.
- By selling investments that have declined in value, the investor can use the losses to counterbalance the capital gains, potentially reducing or even eliminating the taxes owed on those gains.

- **Applying Losses to Ordinary Income**

- If the total losses from tax-loss harvesting exceed the total capital gains for the year, the excess losses can be used to offset ordinary income, such as salary or interest income.
- In many countries, there is a limit to the amount of losses that can be used to offset ordinary income in a single tax year.

- **Reinvesting the Proceeds**

- After selling the investments to realize the losses, the investor can reinvest the proceeds in similar assets or in a different investment.
- It's crucial to avoid running afoul of the "wash-sale rule,"

which disallows a loss deduction if substantially identical securities are repurchased within 30 days before or after the sale.

- **Benefits of Tax-Loss Harvesting**

- Reduced Tax Liability: Tax-loss harvesting can lead to a lower tax bill, allowing investors to keep more of their investment gains.
- Rebalancing Opportunity: While primarily a tax-saving strategy, tax-loss harvesting also creates an opportunity to rebalance the portfolio by reinvesting in assets that align with the investor's long-term goals.

- **Considerations**

- Netting Rules: In some countries, tax laws have specific rules for netting gains and losses from different types of investments. It's important to understand these rules to maximize the tax benefits of harvesting losses.
- Future Tax Implications: While tax-loss harvesting can provide immediate tax benefits, it's essential to consider the potential impact on future tax liabilities. Realized losses today may result in smaller losses available for future tax deductions.

- **Automation**
    - Some online brokerage platforms offer automated tax-loss harvesting services for their clients. These services automatically identify tax-loss harvesting opportunities and execute the necessary trades to optimize tax efficiency.
- **Long-Term Benefits**

    - Tax-loss harvesting is most effective when used as part of a long-term tax strategy. Repeatedly employing the strategy over many years can compound the tax benefits and enhance overall after-tax returns.

Tax-loss harvesting can be a valuable tool for investors, but it should be approached with a thoughtful and strategic mindset. It's essential to work with a qualified tax advisor or financial professional to ensure that tax-loss harvesting aligns with an investor's overall financial goals and tax situation. By employing this technique prudently, investors can enhance their tax efficiency and make the most of their investment portfolio.

Seeking Professional Advice for Complex Tax Situations

Navigating complex tax situations requires a deep understanding of tax laws, regulations, and individual circumstances. In such cases, seeking professional advice from qualified tax advisors or financial professionals is crucial. Here are some scenarios where professional advice can be particularly beneficial:

- **High Net Worth Individuals**

- High net worth individuals often have diverse investment portfolios, complex income sources, and estate planning considerations.
- Tax advisors can provide personalized strategies to optimize tax efficiency, minimize tax liabilities, and align investments with long-term financial goals.

- **Business Owners and Entrepreneurs**

- Business owners and entrepreneurs face unique tax challenges

related to business income, deductions, employee benefits, and business structure.
- Tax professionals can advise on tax planning, compliance, and strategies for reinvesting profits to optimize tax outcomes.

- **International Investments and Taxation**

- Investing in foreign markets can introduce complex tax implications, including foreign tax credits, withholding taxes, and reporting requirements.
- Tax advisors with expertise in international taxation can ensure compliance with applicable tax laws and optimize cross-border investment strategies.

- **Tax-Efficient Retirement Planning**

- Planning for retirement involves various tax-advantaged accounts, Social Security strategies, and tax implications of different retirement income sources.
- Financial professionals can help design retirement plans that maximize tax benefits while ensuring sufficient income during retirement.

- **Estate and Gift Tax Planning**

- Estate planning involves complex tax considerations, such as estate tax exemptions, gift tax rules, and the use of trusts and charitable giving.
- Estate planning attorneys and tax advisors can help create estate plans that minimize estate taxes and efficiently transfer wealth to beneficiaries.

- **Tax Law Changes and Updates**

- Tax laws and regulations change frequently, impacting various investment strategies and financial planning decisions.
- Professional tax advisors stay informed about the latest tax developments and can provide guidance on adapting investment strategies to new tax laws.

- **Tax Compliance for Complex Investments**

- Investors with complex investment vehicles, such as hedge funds, private equity, or venture capital, may have intricate tax reporting requirements.
- Tax professionals with experience in these areas can ensure accurate and timely tax reporting.

- **Tax Controversies and Audits**
    - If an investor is facing a tax audit or controversy, seeking advice from a tax professional can help navigate the process and address potential issues.
- **Minimizing Tax Errors and Penalties**
    - Professional tax advisors can help prevent common tax errors, ensure compliance with tax laws, and minimize the risk of penalties and interest.

In complex tax situations, professional advice can provide significant value by helping investors make well-informed decisions, optimize tax strategies, and avoid costly mistakes. Tax advisors and financial professionals bring expertise and experience to address individual financial circumstances, enabling investors to achieve their financial goals while remaining compliant with tax regulations. When in doubt or when faced with intricate tax scenarios, consulting with a qualified tax advisor is a prudent step towards making sound financial decisions.

Chapter 8: Handling Market Volatility and Risk Management

Emotions and Biases in Investing Decisions

Emotions and cognitive biases can significantly influence investment decisions, often leading to suboptimal outcomes. Understanding these psychological factors can help investors make more rational and disciplined choices. Here are some common emotions and biases that impact investing decisions:

- **Fear and Greed**

- Fear: During periods of market volatility or economic uncertainty, fear can drive investors to sell their investments hastily, attempting to avoid further losses.
- Greed: On the other hand, during bull markets, greed can lead investors to take excessive risks and chase high returns without considering the underlying fundamentals.

- **Loss Aversion**

- Loss aversion is the tendency for individuals to feel the pain of losses more intensely than the pleasure of gains.
- As a result, investors may hold on to losing investments in the hope of recouping losses, even when it is not in their best financial interest.

- **Confirmation Bias**

- Confirmation bias occurs when investors seek information that supports their existing beliefs while ignoring or dismissing contradictory evidence.

- This bias can lead to a skewed perception of investments and hinder a well-rounded analysis.

- **Overconfidence**

- Overconfidence bias can lead investors to overestimate their own abilities and make overly optimistic predictions about the future performance of investments.
- This bias can result in taking excessive risks or failing to diversify adequately.

- **Anchoring**

- Anchoring bias occurs when investors fixate on a particular piece of information, such as the purchase price of an investment, and use it as a reference point for future decisions.
- This can lead to holding onto investments that are no longer favorable based on current market conditions.

- **Herd Mentality**

- The herd mentality is the tendency for individuals to follow the crowd and imitate the actions of others, especially during times of market euphoria or panic.
- This can lead to herd behavior, where investors buy or sell en masse, regardless of the underlying fundamentals.

- **Recency Bias**

- Recency bias is the tendency to give more weight to recent events or information when making decisions.
- Investors may place too much emphasis on recent market

performance and extrapolate short-term trends into the future.

- **Sunk Cost Fallacy**

- The sunk cost fallacy is the tendency to continue investing in a losing position because of the resources (time, money, effort) already invested.
- Investors may be reluctant to cut their losses and sell a declining investment, hoping that it will eventually recover.

- **Regret Aversion**

- Regret aversion occurs when investors avoid making decisions that could lead to regret, even if those decisions are rational and sound.
- This aversion to regret can lead to inaction and missed investment opportunities.

- **Availability Heuristic**

- The availability heuristic is the tendency to rely on readily available information or recent experiences when making judgments.
- Investors may base decisions on recent market events or high-profile news, even if those events are not representative of long-term market behavior.

Being aware of these emotions and biases can help investors recognize when they are influencing their decisions. Developing a disciplined investment strategy, setting clear financial goals, and working with a financial advisor can help mitigate the impact of emotions and biases on investment choices. By maintaining a rational and long-term perspective, investors can make more informed decisions aligned with their financial objectives.

Strategies to Stay Calm During Market Downturns

Market downturns are a natural part of investing, but they can trigger anxiety and fear among investors. Staying calm during turbulent times is essential for making rational decisions and avoiding impulsive actions that may harm long-term financial goals. Here are some strategies to help investors stay composed during market downturns:

- **1. Maintain a Long-Term Perspective**
    - Remember that investing is a journey, and markets experience fluctuations over time. Focus on long-term financial goals rather than short-term market movements.
- **2. Diversify Your Portfolio**

- Diversification spreads risk across different asset classes and investments, reducing the impact of a single investment's downturn on your overall portfolio.
- A well-diversified portfolio is better equipped to weather market turbulence.

- **3. Stick to Your Investment Plan**

- Develop a well-thought-out investment plan that aligns with your risk tolerance and financial objectives.
- Avoid making knee-jerk reactions based on short-term market movements. Stick to your plan, unless there are significant changes in your financial situation or goals.

- **4. Focus on Fundamentals**

- Rely on fundamental analysis rather than emotions or media headlines to make investment decisions.
- Assess the underlying value and prospects of your investments rather than getting swayed by market noise.

- **5. Set Realistic Expectations**

- Acknowledge that markets go through cycles, and there will be periods of volatility and downturns.
- Be prepared for market fluctuations and set realistic return expectations for your investments.

- **6. Limit Information Overload**

- Constantly monitoring financial news and market updates can amplify stress during market downturns.
- While staying informed is essential, avoid excessive exposure to media that may fuel panic.

- **7. Avoid Timing the Market**

- Trying to time the market and predict the bottom or top of a downturn is extremely difficult and risky.
- It's often better to stay invested and ride out market volatility rather than attempting to time market movements.

- **8. Rebalance Your Portfolio**

- Regularly review and rebalance your portfolio to maintain your desired asset allocation.
- Rebalancing involves selling assets that have performed well and buying those that have underperformed, which can be a disciplined approach during downturns.

- **9. Seek Professional Guidance**

- If you find market volatility overwhelming, consider seeking advice from a qualified financial advisor.
- A financial advisor can provide personalized guidance, offer reassurance, and help you make informed decisions.

- **10. Maintain Adequate Cash Reserves**

- Having an emergency fund and adequate cash reserves can provide a sense of security during uncertain times.
- Knowing that you have sufficient funds to cover immediate expenses can reduce anxiety related to market downturns.

- **11. Focus on Quality Investments**

- Invest in fundamentally strong companies and assets that have a history of weathering market downturns.
- High-quality investments are more likely to recover and provide long-term value.

By employing these strategies, investors can better navigate market downturns with a calm and rational mindset. Remember that investing involves both ups and downs, and staying disciplined during challenging times can contribute to long-term investment success.

The Importance of Diversification and Risk Management

Diversification and risk management are essential principles in investing that help protect and optimize investment portfolios. They play a crucial role in managing uncertainty and volatility in financial markets. Here's why diversification and risk management are so important:

- **1. Spreading Risk**

- Diversification involves investing in a wide range of assets, industries, and geographic regions.
- By spreading investments across various assets, the impact of a decline in any single investment is mitigated.

- **2. Reducing Portfolio Volatility**

- Different assets may respond differently to market events. When one asset class declines, another may rise or remain stable.
- A well-diversified portfolio tends to exhibit lower volatility compared to concentrated portfolios.

- **3. Enhancing Risk-Adjusted Returns**

- Diversification can improve the risk-adjusted returns of a portfolio.
- By achieving a balance between risk and return, investors can optimize their chances of meeting financial goals without taking excessive risks.

- **4. Managing Systematic and Unsystematic Risk**

- Systematic risk, also known as market risk, affects the entire market and cannot be eliminated through diversification. Examples include economic downturns and geopolitical events.
- Unsystematic risk, also known as specific or diversifiable risk, is unique to individual assets or industries and can be reduced through diversification.

- **5. Hedging Against Unexpected Events**

- Diversification can act as a hedge against unexpected events that impact specific industries or sectors.
- A well-diversified portfolio is better prepared to weather sudden changes in market conditions.

- **6. Protecting Capital**

- Preservation of capital is a fundamental principle of risk management.
- Diversification helps safeguard the value of a portfolio, reducing the risk of significant losses.

- **7. Balancing Income and Growth Objectives**

- Diversified portfolios can balance the need for income and growth by including assets with different risk-return profiles.
- Some assets, such as dividend-paying stocks or bonds, may provide income, while others, like growth stocks, may offer potential for capital appreciation.

- **8. Adapting to Changing Market Conditions**

- Market conditions can be dynamic and subject to shifts over time.
- Diversification allows investors to adapt to changing economic and market environments.

- **9. Reducing Behavioral Biases**

- Diversification can help reduce the impact of behavioral biases, such as overconfidence or loss aversion, by providing a disciplined investment approach.

- A well-diversified portfolio encourages investors to focus on the long-term rather than reacting impulsively to short-term market movements.

- **10. Aligning with Risk Tolerance**

- Diversification allows investors to customize their portfolio to match their risk tolerance and investment objectives.
- It helps strike a balance between seeking growth and managing risk in a way that aligns with individual preferences.

Overall, diversification and risk management are vital tools in building resilient and successful investment portfolios. By embracing these principles, investors can navigate market volatility with more confidence and stay on track towards their financial goals.

Hedging Techniques to Protect Your Portfolio

Hedging is a risk management strategy used to protect a portfolio from potential losses in the face of adverse market movements. While it may not eliminate all risk, hedging can serve as an insurance policy to limit the impact of market downturns. Here are some common hedging techniques to protect your portfolio:

- **1. Diversification**
    - As mentioned earlier, diversification is a fundamental form of hedging. Spreading investments across various asset classes, industries, and geographic regions can reduce the impact of losses from any single investment.
- **2. Asset Allocation**

- Adjusting your asset allocation to be more conservative can act as a hedge during times of increased market volatility or when approaching specific financial goals.
- For example, shifting a portion of the portfolio into more stable assets, such as bonds or cash, can provide a buffer against market downturns.

- **3. Protective Put Options**

- Buying put options on individual stocks or market indexes allows investors to protect their positions against potential declines in value.
- A put option gives the holder the right to sell an asset at a specified price within a defined time frame, providing downside protection.

- **4. Stop-Loss Orders**

- Placing stop-loss orders on individual investments sets a predetermined price at which the investment will be sold automatically if it reaches that level.
- Stop-loss orders help limit losses on specific positions by enforcing a disciplined approach to selling when a certain threshold is breached.

- **5. Long-Term Government Bonds**

- During times of market uncertainty, long-term government bonds tend to act as a safe-haven asset.
- Investing in government bonds can provide stability and income during volatile market conditions.

- **6. Inverse Exchange-Traded Funds (ETFs)**

- Inverse ETFs are designed to deliver the opposite performance of a particular index or asset.
- Investing in inverse ETFs can generate gains when the underlying market experiences losses, acting as a hedge against downturns.

- **7. Gold and Precious Metals**

- Gold and other precious metals are often considered safe-haven assets that tend to hold value during market turmoil.
- Allocating a portion of the portfolio to gold or precious metals can serve as a hedge against economic uncertainty and inflation.

- **8. Tactical Asset Allocation**

- Tactical asset allocation involves making strategic adjustments to the portfolio based on current market conditions and economic outlook.
- By dynamically adjusting asset allocation, investors can take advantage of potential opportunities or reduce exposure to perceived risks.

- **9. Tail Risk Hedging**

- Tail risk hedging involves using complex financial instruments or strategies to protect against extreme market events or "tail risks."
- These strategies may include options-based hedges or dynamic hedging techniques.

- **10. Risk Parity**

- Risk parity is an approach to portfolio construction that aims to balance risk equally across different asset classes.
- This strategy can provide a more balanced risk profile, reducing vulnerability to specific market movements.

It's important to note that while hedging can protect against certain risks, it may also introduce costs and limit potential upside gains. Additionally, hedging requires a good understanding of the hedging instruments and the market dynamics involved. Investors should carefully consider their risk tolerance, investment goals, and consult with a qualified financial advisor before implementing hedging strategies.

Chapter 9: Long-Term Investment Approaches

Value Investing vs. Growth Investing

Value investing and growth investing are two distinct long-term investment approaches that have been popularized by prominent investors and have different philosophies when it comes to selecting investments. Each approach has its own set of characteristics and considerations. Let's explore the key differences between value investing and growth investing:

- **Value Investing**

- **Philosophy**: Value investing is based on the principle of identifying undervalued assets in the market. The central idea is to find investments that are trading at a price lower than their intrinsic value.
- **Investment Selection**: Value investors look for stocks or assets that they believe the market has underestimated or overlooked, leading to a lower market price than what the asset is truly worth.
- **Financial Metrics**: Value investors often analyze financial metrics such as price-to-earnings (P/E) ratio, price-to-book (P/B) ratio, and dividend yield to identify undervalued stocks.
- **Dividends**: Value stocks, being typically more established and stable companies, tend to pay dividends, making them attractive to income-oriented investors.
- **Investor Behavior**: Value investing requires patience, as it may take time for the market to recognize the true value of

the investment.

- **Growth Investing**

- **Philosophy**: Growth investing centers around identifying companies with strong growth potential and prospects for expanding their earnings at an above-average rate compared to the overall market.
- **Investment Selection**: Growth investors seek out companies that are expected to experience significant revenue and earnings growth in the future. These companies may reinvest profits into expanding their operations rather than paying dividends.
- **Financial Metrics**: Growth investors often focus on metrics such as revenue growth, earnings growth, and projected future earnings to assess a company's potential.
- **Risk**: Growth stocks can be riskier because they often trade at higher valuations, reflecting investors' optimistic expectations for future growth.
- **Investor Behavior**: Growth investing typically requires a higher tolerance for volatility, as these stocks may experience significant price swings in response to changes in growth expectations.

- **Complementary Approaches**:

- While value investing and growth investing have different philosophies, some investors choose to combine elements of both approaches in their portfolios.
- Some investment strategies, known as "blend" or "core" strategies, aim to strike a balance between value and growth by including a mix of value and growth stocks.

- **Market Conditions**:

- The performance of value and growth stocks can be cyclical, with periods of outperformance for each style depending on market conditions and economic cycles.
- For example, value stocks may perform well during economic recoveries, while growth stocks may excel during periods of strong economic expansion.

- **Long-Term Perspective**:

- Both value and growth investing are long-term strategies that require discipline and patience.
- Investors should consider their risk tolerance, investment goals, and time horizon when deciding which approach aligns best with their financial objectives.

It's essential to remember that no investment approach is foolproof, and diversification remains a key element of a well-balanced portfolio. Some investors may choose to incorporate both value and growth investments to create a diversified portfolio that takes advantage of opportunities from both styles. Additionally, individual stocks and companies should be thoroughly researched and analyzed to ensure they align with the investor's overall strategy and risk tolerance.

Dividend Investing and Its Benefits

Dividend investing is an investment approach that focuses on selecting stocks or other assets from companies that regularly pay dividends to their shareholders. Dividends are a portion of a company's profits distributed to its shareholders, typically in the form of cash payments. Dividend investing offers several benefits for investors:

- **1. Income Generation**

- Dividend investing provides a reliable income stream for investors, especially those seeking regular cash flow in addition to potential capital appreciation.
- Dividend payments can serve as a source of passive income, making dividend stocks attractive to income-oriented investors, retirees, and those seeking financial stability.

- **2. Stability and Lower Volatility**

- Dividend-paying stocks often come from well-established and financially stable companies with a history of generating steady earnings.
- During market downturns, dividend stocks may demonstrate more resilience and lower volatility compared to non-dividend-paying stocks, providing a cushion against market turbulence.

- **3. Long-Term Performance**

- Historically, dividend-paying stocks have shown competitive long-term performance, with dividend reinvestment leading to compounding returns over time.
- Reinvesting dividends allows investors to benefit from the power of compounding, potentially increasing the overall return on investment.

- **4. Discipline and Quality**

- Companies that consistently pay dividends demonstrate financial discipline and stability.
- Dividend payments can signal a company's confidence in its future prospects and commitment to returning value to shareholders.

- **5. Tax Advantages**

- In many countries, dividend income is often taxed at a lower rate than ordinary income, providing a tax advantage for dividend investors.
- Additionally, some tax-advantaged accounts, such as Roth IRAs, allow investors to receive tax-free dividends in retirement.

- **6. Diversification**

- Dividend investing can offer diversification benefits, as dividend-paying companies span various industries and sectors.
- Investors can build a diversified dividend portfolio that may be less susceptible to industry-specific risks.

- **7. Focus on Value**

- Dividend investing often aligns with a value-oriented approach, as investors seek out companies with solid fundamentals and reasonable valuations.
- This focus on value can provide a margin of safety for investors, especially during market downturns.

- **8. Inflation Hedge**
    - Dividend payments can act as a hedge against inflation, as companies may increase dividends over time to keep up with rising prices.
- **9. Reinvestment Flexibility**
    - Investors have the option to reinvest dividends to acquire more shares of the dividend-paying stock or use the cash for other investment opportunities.

- **10. Lower Dependency on Market Timing**
    - Dividend income is relatively independent of short-term market movements, allowing investors to rely on the regular income stream without timing the market.

It's important to note that dividend investing is not without risks. Some companies may reduce or suspend dividend payments during challenging economic conditions or periods of financial distress. Therefore, investors should conduct thorough research and analysis of dividend-paying companies to ensure their sustainability and growth potential. Additionally, diversification remains critical, and investors may choose to complement dividend stocks with other investment strategies to create a well-rounded portfolio that aligns with their financial goals and risk tolerance.

Contrarian Investing and Buying Opportunities During Market Panics

Contrarian investing is an investment strategy that involves going against prevailing market sentiment and making decisions that are opposite to the popular consensus. Contrarian investors believe that markets can be driven by emotions and that opportunities arise when market participants overreact to news or events. During market panics and downturns, contrarian investors actively seek buying opportunities. Here's how contrarian investing works and its benefits:

- **1. Going Against the Crowd**

- Contrarian investors avoid following the herd mentality and do not get swept up in market euphoria or panic.
- They are willing to take positions that differ from the prevailing market sentiment, which can lead to uncovering

undervalued assets.

- **2. Buying During Market Panics**

- Market panics, characterized by sharp declines in asset prices, can create attractive buying opportunities for contrarian investors.
- During panics, many assets may be oversold and trading at prices significantly below their intrinsic value.

- **3. Capitalizing on Market Overreactions**

- Contrarian investors believe that markets can overreact to both positive and negative news, leading to exaggerated price movements.
- They seek to take advantage of these overreactions to find assets trading at attractive entry points.

- **4. Long-Term Perspective**

- Contrarian investing is a long-term approach that requires patience and conviction in the underlying value of investments.
- Contrarian investors often have the confidence to hold positions while waiting for the market to recognize the assets' true worth.

- **5. Buying Quality Assets at a Discount**

- Contrarian investors look for fundamentally strong assets with promising growth prospects that have temporarily fallen out of favor in the market.
- By purchasing quality assets at discounted prices, contrarians

position themselves for potential gains when sentiment improves.

- **6. Avoiding Herd Behavior**

- Contrarian investing helps investors avoid the pitfalls of herd behavior, where fear or greed leads to irrational decision-making.
- By maintaining independent thinking, contrarian investors can stay disciplined and make rational choices based on fundamentals.

- **7. Risk Management**

- Contrarian investors pay attention to risk management and position sizing to limit potential losses in case their analysis is incorrect.
- They may diversify across different assets and sectors to spread risk.

- **8. Capitalizing on Market Cycles**

- Contrarian investing aligns with the concept of market cycles, where sentiment shifts from optimism to pessimism and back again.
- By buying during times of pessimism, contrarians position themselves to benefit from potential future market recoveries.

- **9. Fundamental Analysis**

- Contrarian investors heavily rely on fundamental analysis to identify undervalued assets.
- They assess financial metrics, earnings potential, and

company fundamentals to make informed investment decisions.

- **10. Emotional Discipline**

- Contrarian investing requires emotional discipline to avoid being swayed by short-term market fluctuations or negative sentiment.
- Sticking to a well-thought-out investment strategy is crucial for long-term success.

Contrarian investing can be rewarding, but it is not without risks. Markets may continue to be pessimistic for extended periods, and not all contrarian bets will turn out to be profitable. As with any investment strategy, thorough research and analysis are essential, and diversification can help mitigate specific risks associated with contrarian positions. Investors considering this approach should have a deep understanding of the assets they are investing in and be prepared to hold their positions patiently until the market sentiment aligns with their investment thesis.

Understanding the Role of a Financial Advisor, if Needed

A financial advisor is a professional who provides expert guidance and advice on various aspects of personal finance, including investing, retirement planning, tax strategies, risk management, and more. While individuals can manage their investments independently, working with a financial advisor can offer several benefits and play a crucial role in achieving long-term financial success. Here's an understanding of the role of a financial advisor:

- **1. Personalized Financial Planning**

- A financial advisor works with clients to develop a

comprehensive financial plan tailored to their specific goals, needs, and risk tolerance.
- The plan considers various aspects of the individual's financial life, such as budgeting, saving, investing, and retirement planning.

- **2. Investment Guidance**

- A financial advisor assists in constructing an investment portfolio aligned with the client's financial objectives and time horizon.
- They consider factors like asset allocation, diversification, risk management, and selecting appropriate investment vehicles.

- **3. Objective Advice**

- Financial advisors provide objective advice that is not influenced by emotions or biases.
- They analyze market trends, economic conditions, and individual circumstances to make well-informed and unbiased recommendations.

- **4. Monitoring and Rebalancing**

- A financial advisor continuously monitors the client's portfolio performance and market conditions.
- They may recommend adjustments or rebalancing to keep the portfolio aligned with the client's goals and risk tolerance.

- **5. Retirement Planning**

- Financial advisors help clients create retirement plans that ensure they have sufficient savings to meet their lifestyle and financial needs during retirement.

- They consider factors like Social Security optimization, pension options, and tax-efficient withdrawal strategies.

- **6. Tax Efficiency**
    - Financial advisors help clients minimize their tax burden through strategies like tax-loss harvesting, utilizing tax-advantaged accounts, and optimizing tax deductions.
- **7. Risk Management and Insurance**

- Financial advisors assess the client's insurance needs and recommend appropriate coverage to protect against unforeseen events.
- This may include life insurance, disability insurance, long-term care insurance, and liability coverage.

- **8. Estate Planning**
    - Financial advisors work with clients to create estate plans that include wills, trusts, and other legal documents to ensure the smooth transfer of assets to heirs and beneficiaries.
- **9. Behavioral Coaching**

- Financial advisors provide behavioral coaching to help clients stay disciplined during market volatility and avoid emotional investment decisions.
- They act as a source of support and guidance, particularly during challenging market conditions.

- **10. Financial Education**

- Financial advisors educate clients about various financial concepts, investment strategies, and the implications of different financial decisions.

- Empowering clients with financial knowledge helps them make well-informed choices and develop a stronger financial foundation.

While financial advisors offer valuable expertise and personalized guidance, it's essential to choose a qualified professional who acts in the client's best interest. Look for advisors with relevant credentials, experience, and a fiduciary duty, meaning they are legally obligated to put their clients' interests first. Conduct due diligence, seek referrals, and have an open and transparent discussion about fees and services before engaging a financial advisor. Working with a trusted and competent advisor can enhance an investor's financial journey and help them navigate complex financial landscapes with confidence.

Chapter 10: Reviewing Your Portfolio and Making Adjustments

The Significance of Regular Portfolio Reviews

Regular portfolio reviews are a critical aspect of successful long-term investing. They involve assessing the performance and composition of your investment portfolio at regular intervals. The frequency of reviews can vary depending on individual preferences, but generally, conducting them annually or semi-annually is a common practice. Here's why regular portfolio reviews are significant:

- **1. Performance Evaluation**

- Portfolio reviews allow you to evaluate the performance of your investments over a specific period.
- By comparing your actual returns to your investment objectives, you can assess whether your portfolio is on track to meet your financial goals.

- **2. Rebalancing and Asset Allocation**

- Over time, the value of different assets in your portfolio may change, altering your asset allocation.
- Portfolio reviews provide an opportunity to rebalance your portfolio by adjusting the allocation of assets back to your desired targets.
- Rebalancing ensures that your risk exposure aligns with your risk tolerance and long-term objectives.

- **3. Addressing Changes in Risk Tolerance**

- Life circumstances and risk tolerance may change over time.

- A portfolio review allows you to assess whether your investments still align with your current risk tolerance and financial situation.
- If needed, adjustments can be made to ensure your portfolio reflects your current preferences and circumstances.

- **4. Identifying Underperforming Assets**

- Portfolio reviews help you identify underperforming assets or investments that are not meeting your expectations.
- If certain investments consistently lag behind, you may consider replacing them with potentially more promising options.

- **5. Taking Advantage of New Opportunities**

- Market conditions, economic outlook, and investment opportunities are continually evolving.
- Regular portfolio reviews enable you to assess whether there are new investment opportunities that fit your strategy and long-term goals.

- **6. Tax Planning**

- Portfolio reviews provide an opportunity for tax planning.
- You can assess the tax implications of potential changes to your portfolio and identify strategies to minimize tax liabilities.

- **7. Adapting to Economic Changes**

- Economic conditions can have a significant impact on investment performance.

- By reviewing your portfolio, you can make adjustments to align with changing economic trends and potential shifts in market dynamics.

- **8. Staying Disciplined**

- Regular portfolio reviews encourage disciplined investing.
- They help you avoid making impulsive decisions based on short-term market movements and reinforce a long-term perspective.

- **9. Financial Goal Adjustments**

- As your financial goals evolve or change, your portfolio may need to be adjusted accordingly.
- Portfolio reviews facilitate aligning your investments with your updated financial objectives.

- **10. Peace of Mind**

- Knowing that your portfolio is being regularly reviewed and adjusted as needed can provide peace of mind.
- You can be confident that your investments are being actively managed to optimize their potential for long-term growth.

Portfolio reviews are not about making constant changes or trying to time the market. Instead, they are about maintaining a disciplined approach to investing, ensuring that your investments remain aligned with your financial goals and risk tolerance. If you are unsure about how to conduct a portfolio review or make adjustments, seeking the guidance of a financial advisor can be beneficial. A qualified advisor can help you navigate the review process and make informed decisions that align with your long-term financial objectives.

Rebalancing Your Portfolio to Maintain Desired Asset Allocation

Rebalancing is the process of realigning your investment portfolio back to its original target asset allocation. Over time, the performance of different assets can cause your portfolio's allocation to deviate from your initial strategy. Rebalancing helps ensure that your portfolio remains consistent with your risk tolerance and long-term goals. Here's why rebalancing is essential and how it can be done effectively:

- **1. Risk Management**

- Rebalancing helps manage risk by preventing your portfolio from becoming too heavily weighted in a particular asset class or investment.
- Without rebalancing, an overexposure to certain assets could lead to increased volatility and potential losses during market downturns.

- **2. Asset Allocation Alignment**

- Over time, the value of different assets will grow at different rates, causing your asset allocation to drift from its original targets.
- Rebalancing brings your asset allocation back to the desired percentages, ensuring it aligns with your risk profile and investment strategy.

- **3. Buy Low, Sell High**

- Rebalancing inherently involves selling assets that have outperformed and buying those that have underperformed.
- This "buy low, sell high" approach helps investors take profits from assets that have done well and reinvest in assets that may

have better growth potential.

- **4. Long-Term Strategy Reinforcement**

- Rebalancing reinforces your long-term investment strategy by keeping you disciplined and preventing emotional reactions to market fluctuations.
- It encourages you to maintain a consistent approach to investing regardless of short-term market movements.

- **5. Regular Interval vs. Threshold-Based Rebalancing**

- Rebalancing can be done at regular intervals (e.g., annually or semi-annually) or when certain thresholds are breached.
- Regular interval rebalancing provides a disciplined approach, while threshold-based rebalancing is triggered when the asset allocation deviates beyond a set percentage (e.g., 5% from the target).

- **6. Consider Tax Implications**

- When rebalancing a taxable account, be mindful of potential tax consequences.
- Selling appreciated assets may generate capital gains taxes, which can impact your overall tax liability.

- **7. Incremental Adjustments**

- In some cases, you may choose to rebalance gradually by making small adjustments over time instead of large, sudden changes.
- This approach can be useful if you want to avoid market timing or if transaction costs are a concern.

- **8. Reassessing Your Investment Strategy**

- When rebalancing, take the opportunity to review your investment strategy and assess whether it aligns with your current financial goals and risk tolerance.
- Adjust your strategy if necessary to ensure it reflects your evolving circumstances.

- **9. Use New Contributions**

- If you regularly contribute to your portfolio, consider using new contributions to rebalance rather than making additional trades.
- This can help minimize transaction costs and keep your portfolio on track.

- **10. Seek Professional Advice**

- If you are unsure about the best approach to rebalancing or need help with the process, consult with a financial advisor.
- A qualified advisor can provide personalized guidance and tailor the rebalancing strategy to your specific needs and circumstances.

Rebalancing is an essential aspect of portfolio management, as it ensures that your investments remain aligned with your financial objectives and risk tolerance. By periodically reviewing and rebalancing your portfolio, you can maintain a well-structured and disciplined investment approach that enhances the potential for long-term success.

Adjusting Your Investment Strategy as Life Circumstances Change

Life circumstances, such as major life events or changes in financial goals, can significantly impact your investment strategy. As you move through different stages of life, it's essential to reassess your investment approach and make necessary adjustments to ensure that your portfolio remains aligned with your evolving needs. Here's why adjusting your investment strategy is crucial and how to do it effectively:

- **1. Changing Financial Goals**

- As your financial goals change over time, so should your investment strategy.
- Different life stages, such as starting a family, buying a home, or planning for retirement, may require adjustments to the risk level and time horizon of your investments.

- **2. Risk Tolerance**

- Major life events or changes in your financial situation can impact your risk tolerance.
- Assess your comfort level with risk periodically and adjust your portfolio to match your current risk tolerance.

- **3. Time Horizon**

- Your investment time horizon influences the appropriate asset allocation and investment choices.
- Shorter-term goals may call for more conservative investments, while long-term goals may warrant a more growth-oriented strategy.

- **4. Retirement Planning**

- As you approach retirement, your investment focus may shift from accumulation to income generation and capital preservation.

- Consider adjusting your portfolio to emphasize assets that can provide reliable income during retirement.

- **5. Regular Financial Checkups**

- Conduct regular financial checkups to evaluate your overall financial health and assess whether your investments align with your financial plan.
- A comprehensive review can help identify areas where adjustments are needed.

- **6. Consider Changes in Income**

- Changes in your income, such as salary increases or decreases, can impact your ability to save and invest.
- Adjust your investment contributions and strategies to accommodate changes in cash flow.

- **7. Tax Considerations**

- Changes in your tax situation, such as changes in tax laws or your income level, may require adjustments to tax-efficient investment strategies.
- Consult with a tax advisor to optimize your investment plan from a tax perspective.

- **8. Estate Planning**

- As your wealth grows, estate planning becomes increasingly important.
- Review your estate plan regularly and ensure that your investment strategy aligns with your estate planning goals.

- **9. Flexibility and Adaptability**

- An effective investment strategy should be flexible and adaptable to changing market conditions and life events.
- Be prepared to adjust your strategy as needed to navigate economic uncertainties and take advantage of new opportunities.

- **10. Seek Professional Guidance**

- Making significant adjustments to your investment strategy can be complex and may require professional guidance.
- Work with a financial advisor to develop a customized plan that addresses your unique financial situation and goals.

Adjusting your investment strategy in response to life circumstances is essential for maintaining financial stability and pursuing your long-term objectives. Life is dynamic, and your investment approach should be dynamic as well. Regularly review your investment strategy, seek professional advice when needed, and make informed decisions that align with your evolving financial journey.

Looking Ahead: Retirement Planning and Wealth Preservation

As you progress through life and accumulate wealth, it becomes increasingly important to focus on retirement planning and wealth preservation. Retirement planning involves preparing for your financial needs after you stop working, while wealth preservation aims to protect and grow your assets to ensure a comfortable and secure future. Here's why retirement planning and wealth preservation are vital and some key considerations for these stages:

- **1. Retirement Goals and Lifestyle**

- Define your retirement goals and the lifestyle you envision during your post-work years.
- Estimate your expected retirement expenses, taking into account factors such as housing, healthcare, travel, and other essential living costs.

- **2. Retirement Savings and Investments**

- Assess your current retirement savings and investment accounts.
- Determine if your current contributions and investment returns are sufficient to meet your retirement objectives.

- **3. Retirement Account Options**

- Familiarize yourself with various retirement accounts, such as 401(k)s, IRAs, Roth IRAs, and pension plans.
- Maximize contributions to tax-advantaged retirement accounts to benefit from potential tax savings and compounding growth.

- **4. Asset Allocation in Retirement**

- Adjust your asset allocation as you approach retirement to reduce exposure to high-risk investments.
- Consider allocating a portion of your portfolio to income-generating assets to meet your retirement income needs.

- **5. Longevity and Healthcare Costs**

- Plan for the possibility of a long retirement and consider the impact of rising healthcare costs as you age.
- Investigate long-term care insurance options to protect

against potential high medical expenses.

- **6. Estate and Legacy Planning**

- Create or update your estate plan to ensure your assets are distributed according to your wishes.
- Review beneficiaries on retirement accounts and insurance policies to keep them current.

- **7. Regular Retirement Projections**

- Regularly project your retirement income and expenses to gauge whether you are on track to achieve your retirement goals.
- Make adjustments to your savings and investment strategy as needed to align with your projections.

- **8. Diversification and Risk Management**
    - Continue to prioritize diversification and risk management to protect your wealth from potential market volatility and economic uncertainties.
- **9. Professional Financial Advice**

- Seeking advice from a financial advisor can be beneficial as you navigate the complexities of retirement planning and wealth preservation.
- A qualified advisor can help you develop a comprehensive retirement strategy and ensure that your financial plan remains on track.

- **10. Focus on Long-Term Goals**

- Stay focused on your long-term financial goals and avoid

making drastic decisions based on short-term market fluctuations.
- A disciplined and patient approach to wealth preservation can lead to sustainable financial security.

Retirement planning and wealth preservation are continuous processes that require proactive management and regular adjustments as circumstances change. By taking a forward-looking approach and implementing a well-structured retirement plan, you can work toward financial independence and enjoy a comfortable retirement. Remember to consider factors like lifestyle goals, healthcare expenses, estate planning, and the guidance of a financial advisor to optimize your strategy and protect your wealth for the future.

Conclusion:

Investing Demystified: A Beginner's Guide to Building Wealth in the Stock Market offers a comprehensive and accessible introduction to the world of investing. Throughout the book, we've explored various essential topics to equip beginners with the knowledge and tools they need to build wealth in the stock market and other assets.

In Chapter 1, we laid the foundation by understanding the significance of investing for one's financial future. We explored the concept of risk and return in different investment vehicles, setting the stage for informed decision-making. Additionally, we provided an overview of stocks, bonds, mutual funds, and other assets, offering a glimpse into the wide array of investment opportunities available.

The power of compounding, introduced in Chapter 1, became a central theme throughout the book. Chapter 2 delved into the world of stocks, explaining their workings and different types, including common and preferred stocks. We explored how to research and select individual stocks, making informed investment decisions.

Chapter 3 introduced bonds and fixed-income investments, highlighting their differences from stocks and understanding bond yields, maturity, and credit ratings. We explored the role of government, corporate, and municipal bonds in a balanced investment portfolio.

Chapter 4 delved into mutual funds and exchange-traded funds (ETFs), emphasizing the benefits of diversification and how to choose the right funds to align with specific investment goals. We explored the impact of expense ratios on investment returns and the importance of keeping costs in check.

Chapter 5 guided readers in building their investment strategy, assessing risk tolerance, and understanding the significance of asset allocation in a portfolio. We compared long-term and short-term investing strategies and explored the advantages of dollar-cost averaging.

In Chapters 6 and 7, we delved into market analysis, investment research, and tax-efficient investing strategies. We explained the fundamentals vs. technical analysis, key financial metrics for stock evaluation, analyzing macroeconomic factors, and utilizing online resources for investment research. Additionally, we explored strategies for tax-efficient investing, including the use of retirement accounts and tax-loss harvesting.

Chapter 8 focused on handling market volatility and risk management, emphasizing the role of emotions and providing strategies to stay calm during market downturns. We explored the importance of diversification and hedging techniques to protect portfolios.

Chapter 9 introduced long-term investment approaches, comparing value investing and growth investing. We explored dividend investing and the benefits of contrarian investing during market panics. Additionally, we discussed the role of a financial advisor and the importance of regular portfolio reviews to make necessary adjustments.

Finally, in Chapter 10, we emphasized the significance of retirement planning and wealth preservation as life circumstances change. We explored the need to adjust investment strategies to align with changing financial goals, risk tolerance, and time horizon.

As readers embark on their investment journey, we encourage them to approach investing with patience, discipline, and a long-term perspective. The world of investing can be both rewarding and challenging, but armed with knowledge and a commitment to sound financial principles, individuals can build wealth and achieve their financial aspirations. Remember, seeking professional advice, staying informed, and continuously learning are essential components of a successful investment journey.

May Investing Demystified serve as a guiding light for beginners, empowering them to confidently navigate the complexities of the stock market and other investment avenues to secure their financial future. Happy investing!

Don't miss out!

Visit the website below and you can sign up to receive emails whenever Alex Thompson publishes a new book. There's no charge and no obligation.

https://books2read.com/r/B-A-FEPY-PNEMC

BOOKS 2 READ

Connecting independent readers to independent writers.

Also by Alex Thompson

Alex on Finance

Financial Freedom Roadmap - Achieving Early Retirement through the FIRE Movement

The Art of Strategic Innovation

Beyond Cash - The Evolution of Digital Payment Systems and the Future of Money

Preserving Wealth in Inflationary Times - Strategies for Protecting Your Financial Future

Standalone

Side Hustle Success: Unlocking Your Entrepreneurial Potential

Side Hustle Success: The Ultimate Guide to Passive and Financial Freedom

Mastering the Markets: Advanced Trading Strategies for Success and Ethical Trading Practices

Financial Fortitude

Mastering the Art of Upselling

The Financial Bullet Blueprint

Investing Demystified: A Beginner's Guide to Building Wealth in the Stock Market

www.ingramcontent.com/pod-product-compliance
Lightning Source LLC
LaVergne TN
LVHW022102200926
848481LV00003B/1034

9798223167303